ANGER

was never the enemy

THE CALL TO COMPASSION WE MISSED

Shuddhaanandaa Brahmachari

LOKENATH DIVINE LIFE MISSION

KOLKATA

Anger Was Never the Enemy
The Call to Compassion We Missed

by Shuddhaanandaa Brahmachari
(Author of *The Incredible Life of a Himalayan Yogi*)

Cover Design and Interior by: TeaBerryStudio.com
Kindle formatting by: Anirban Banerjee and Sue Berg

ISBN: 978-81-982864-0-6

Please send your personal experiences and comments on reading this book to susan@feelinghearts.org, and we will personally answer your email.

DEDICATION

To the Seekers of Peace,

"Anger is a natural human instinct and a defense mechanism. It's normal to feel upset when your expectations or sense of respect are threatened. But when anger becomes chronic—a default reaction to others—it can destroy your peace. The only antidote is to practice calmness through deep breathing, mindful thinking, and compassionate living. Anger may still arise, but it won't possess you anymore. May the Light you become be part of what Heals the world!"

—Bodhi Shuddhaanandaa

ACKNOWLEDGMENT

It is often said that it takes a village to raise a child—and in God's perfect timing, it has taken a dedicated village of seva to bring this book into being.

The seed for this book on anger was planted in March 2024, when Ipsita envisioned transcribing and compiling Bodhi's talks into monthly books. Her dear friend Rajashree in the U.S. took on the heartfelt work of transcribing several talks on anger, while Norman Cat in Chicago contributed valuable Q&A archives from Bodhi's earlier website.

Rajashree completed the initial editing and chapter arrangement, which Bodhi later refined. Yet, as Divine Will would have it, other seva delayed progress until July, when Bodhi declared: "It is time to complete the Anger book before my U.S. tour." With Norman sending chapters daily, the book was rewritten through Bodhi's inspiration, guided by the grace of the Universe and the Great Masters. It expanded to 25 chapters, blending practical tools and timeless wisdom for our world in need of healing.

I offer heartfelt thanks to Ipsita for her vision and leadership; to Sakshi, Maiyatree, and Sugeeti for their support; to Rajashree for her tireless transcription and initial editing; to Norman for organizing and coordinating materials; to Anirban for eBook formatting; and Lisa for her initial cover art. And I offer my deep gratitude to Tara of TeaBerry Creative for her beautiful cover design and interior, which she completed in record time, so this book could be available to all.

May this collaborative effort continue to bear fruit in the form of many more offerings for the upliftment of all.

With gratitude and love,
Shuddhaanandaa Brahmachari (Bodhi)

CONTENTS

PREFACE

In these times of global unrest and personal turmoil, I feel deeply the urgency of inner transformation. Anger, which has become so common in our daily lives, is not our enemy. It is a powerful force that, when understood and transformed, can become a gateway to compassion, strength, and healing.

This small work is a humble offering—born not from any desire to write a book, but from the sincere intention to serve. Over many decades of spiritual practice and sharing, I have witnessed how anger causes suffering and disconnection. Yet, I have also seen how awareness, love, and simple daily practices can restore peace—within ourselves and in the world around us.

My role here is not that of a teacher above others, but a fellow seeker walking with you. These conversations are born from real questions asked by sincere souls, and the answers arise from my heart, guided by the grace of the Masters and the living wisdom of the Universe.

May this offering serve as a gentle companion on your path toward greater self-awareness and peace. If these words inspire even one soul to pause, breathe, and choose love over anger, then this work has fulfilled its purpose.

With deep love and gratitude,
Shuddhaanandaa Brahmachari (Bodhi)

INTRODUCTION

A CONVERSATION WITH BODHI ABOUT ANGER

Have you ever wished to sit before a wise master, asking all your questions until the answers came effortlessly, even without asking? Join this simple yet profound Question-and-Answer session with Karma Yogi Shuddhaanandaa Brahmachari (Bodhi), as he shares his wisdom from the Vedic Masters and his deep interest in both modern neuroscience and psychology, particularly how they intersect in understanding anger.

As Bodhi says:

"Indeed, the world has come a long way in grasping the simpler teachings of Nature and the Universal Mind, expressing them through various platforms and models for the upliftment of millions. This edition wasn't created to write a book or publish it; that was never our goal. Instead, we aimed to explore how, alongside other higher souls working to elevate human consciousness, we could contribute—however modestly—with the same

sublime purpose of Divine Will in action. Anger is not just about the surface-level understanding the masses are often presented with; we seek to explore the deeper intent and purpose behind why the Universe has endowed us with this powerful emotion for our transformative journey. Anger is a vital human emotion, holding within it the seed of potential transformation into love and compassion—something our world needs now more than ever."

Drawing from questions asked by seekers during his Q&A sessions, both online and in live settings worldwide, Bodhi explores how to understand anger, use it as a positive force, and ultimately transform it into compassion and forgiveness in action.

As Bodhi explains, we are composed of different personality traits, or Gunas, which can arise at various times, so there is no one-size-fits-all blueprint for transcending anger. We invite you to explore the questions and practices presented here and to apply whichever suggestions resonate with your unique needs.

With 50 years of experience in mindfulness and meditation, Bodhi weaves his answers in a way that is practical, insightful, and inspiring. His wisdom is here for you whenever a question stirs within your seeking mind.

UNDERSTANDING ANGER, ITS ETIOLOGY AND CHALLENGES

CHAPTER 1
ANGER WAS NEVER THE ENEMY

Q #1: What Is Anger?

Anger is not merely an emotion—it is a deeply rooted pattern within the subconscious mind. It arises from unprocessed pain, unmet needs, and internal conflict. While we often treat it as an enemy, anger is, in its essence, a powerful signal—one that points us toward imbalance, injustice, or unhealed wounds.

To truly overcome anger, one must go beyond psychological effort alone. A complete transformation is only possible through deep connection with the **True Self**, a connection cultivated through **meditation, contemplation, and spiritual practice.** It is through this inner journey that the seed of anger is gradually transmuted into compassion, understanding, and ultimately, joy.

Until one attains this level of spiritual realization, **healthy anger**—the kind that alerts us to wrongs and motivates change—has its role. It is not to be repressed or feared. Repressing anger or other strong emotions may bring temporary silence, but over time, it causes **emotional distortion**, resentment, or self-sabotaging behaviors. Suppression is not peace—it is merely postponement.

Embracing Emotional Awareness

Spirituality is not about bypassing our emotions but about **honoring them** with awareness and compassion. When we allow ourselves to explore our anger with curiosity, we begin to trace it to its origins—often rooted in early pain, fear, or unmet emotional needs. By understanding where it comes from, we begin the sacred work of healing.

This is how instincts evolve into **intuitive insight**. This is how raw emotion becomes refined awareness. This is how the path of spirituality becomes a path of **true self-love and divine connection.**

The Power of Inner Peace

Inner peace is not the absence of triggers—it is the presence of **stillness** in the face of them. It is the space between stimulus and response, where you remain undisturbed, even when the outer world is stormy. This peace comes when you no longer allow provocation to control you, but instead let it pass through you, like wind through open space.

True spiritual maturity lies in your ability to remain **centered, loving, and empathetic**, even in moments of pain or confrontation. This does not mean becoming passive or indifferent, but rather **cultivating a culture of patience, compassion, and understanding** within.

When you endure with the **faith that Universal Intelligence is working through all things**, something miraculous happens: life begins to respond. You find support where you least expect it. You feel held by unseen hands. You experience unexpected sources of love and joy.

In the Eyes of God, You Never Lose

Even when you appear to lose in the outer world, the soul is always gaining. Your growth, your peace, your deepened compassion—these are invisible victories. In the eyes of God, there is no defeat. There is only the unfolding of your higher self, one experience at a time.

In Summary:

- Anger is a subconscious pattern that transforms through spiritual awareness.
- Healthy anger can guide us; repressed anger harms us.
- Emotional awareness is the bridge between instinct and insight.
- Inner peace comes from stillness, not suppression.
- Faith in divine intelligence opens the door to transformation.
- In the spiritual journey, no experience is ever wasted.

Let anger no longer be your enemy. Let it be your teacher—a fire that, when understood, becomes light.

CHAPTER 2
THE SEED OF ANGER LIES WITHIN

Q#2: How can I control my anger in front of the person who is the cause of my anger?

The truth is *that the* person *is not the cause of your anger.* The anger you feel is your own reaction, arising from within you. It is not "them," but *your own practiced habit* of reacting with anger that fuels the fire. Today it is 'X,' tomorrow it will be 'Y,' and the day after, 'Z'—different faces, same reaction—because the *seed of anger* lies buried inside you.

Anyone can provoke that anger if the poison still lingers within you. First, take full ownership. Stop blaming others for what is actually your inner trigger. It is *your beliefs, your perceptions* about the other person, that spark the flame. And when that fire burns, the mind scrambles to find someone *outside* to blame—some object, some person, anything but the self.

People appear in your life to awaken different responses—some bring out your love, others may stir anger, jealousy, or rejection. But all of it is *your interpretation*. Every reaction is born from within you. The external world merely acts as a mirror.

A Point to Ponder

Someone may throw a stone at you, but how you *perceive and respond* is entirely up to you.

Transform that Challenge into Wisdom

"This stone was not thrown at *me;* it was thrown at my *ego.* My true Self cannot be harmed. My soul is like the open sky—throw a stone at the sky, and it remains untouched."

Similarly, people may throw indifference, hurtful words, or actions that defy your expectations. Resist the urge to point fingers—neither at them nor at yourself. Instead, awaken to this truth: **you have developed a habitual pattern of reacting to them.** Your mind, conditioned by past experiences, instantly switches into reaction mode the moment it sees them.

But *you can change that.*

If you change your mindset, even if someone throws a stone, it may touch your body—but not your soul. Like a tortoise that withdraws its limbs in times of threat, you, too, can retreat into your inner stillness. Strike the shell all you want—you won't reach the being within.

No one can truly hurt you unless you allow yourself to be hurt.

As long as you identify with the ego, you will feel wounded. But the moment you awaken to your deeper Self, you become free. You become the same in front of the one who loves you and the one who tests you. Every difficult person is a question the universe poses:

"Are you just your ego, or are you the spirit beyond it?"

Final Reflection

These teachings are not easy to practice—they are elevated truths. But what is the alternative? 'Tit for tat' only keeps the cycle of suffering spinning. You cannot easily change someone locked into their conditioned responses. But you *can* change yourself. And when you do, their behavior will no longer have power over you.

This is an invitation to *look within*. The more we do, the more we shape a world that is calm, peaceful, loving, and wise—a world that reflects the beauty we cultivate inside.

Let this be your path.

CHAPTER 3

EXPLORING THE INTERPLAY OF THOUGHTS AND EMOTIONS

> Q#3: "You often discuss thoughts and how to turn the mind into an ally. But where do feelings and emotions fit into this? I used to believe that all emotions stemmed from thoughts, but now I'm not so sure. Could it be the other way around at times?"

Thoughts and emotions are intricately connected—*two sides of the same coin*. While you may not always be conscious of your thoughts, emotions are much harder to ignore. For instance, when you're overwhelmed with joy, you might not register the thoughts fueling it, but you certainly *feel* the radiance of happiness spreading through your entire being. Thoughts tend to operate in the mind, while emotions express themselves in the body.

Take fear as an example. A sudden surge of fear sends chills down your spine. The body tenses, breath shortens—it feels heavy, suffocating. Or imagine someone hurling an insult that triggers anger. The emotion can hijack your reason before your mind has a chance to catch up, especially if you're unprepared. The mind functions on two planes—it *thinks*, and it *feels*.

Picture this: you're walking peacefully down a forest trail, and suddenly a snake slithers across your path. Your mind flashes an instant thought—*danger*! That thought gives rise to a vivid mental image, while your body simultaneously reacts with fear—racing heart, frozen limbs. Thought and emotion arise together, a tightly knit dance of perception and response.

The Role of Feelings and Emotions in the Divine Scheme

Thoughts arise from the head. Emotions reside in the heart. And in the design of the Divine, it is *the heart*, not the endlessly chattering mind, that is considered the true sanctuary.

At the early stages of spiritual growth, emotions—like anger, fear, jealousy, attachment, and even love—tend to erupt instinctively. They seem automatic, arising without your choosing. However, as the soul evolves through life's trials and awakenings, it begins to recognize the suffering that these lower emotions create. That's when **spiritual Masters** across all traditions begin to call the soul toward *higher ground*—to learn that emotions themselves are not the enemy; they are the fuel for transcendence.

The same emotions that once enslaved the soul—when transformed—can become its wings. Anger redirected can become clarity. Grief refined can deepen compassion. Longing purified becomes devotion. Just as thoughts can either entangle or liberate you, emotions, too, can either bind you to suffering or lift you into *ecstatic communion.*

Even the highest states of spiritual experience—though not emotional in the ordinary sense—are infused with a subtle, sacred form of feeling. Not sentimental, not reactive, but *radiantly alive.*

Let Your Mind Think but Let Your Heart Lead

Thoughts can guide, but feelings—when rooted in wisdom—can transform. The real evolution begins not by silencing emotion, but by sanctifying it. Chant this Mantra Daily:

"Let this be the path forward:
To understand my thoughts, feel my emotions.
To master my emotions, awaken my awareness.
And through awareness, let my being rise in love—
pure, free, and whole."

CHAPTER 4

FROM FIRE TO FREEDOM: THE SACRED WISDOM OF THE MASTERS

Q#4: What Do the Great Spiritual Masters Say About Anger?

In today's world, many of the people we idolize—icons of wealth, fame, and power—have become symbols of a distorted success. They often model aggression, entitlement, and unmindful living, promoting values that pull us away from our inner truth. True icons, however, are the **men and women of wisdom**—those who have walked through the fire of inner struggle and emerged as beacons of light. Their presence doesn't inflame the ego; it awakens the soul.

To transform anger, we must ground ourselves in the **universal laws** taught by these spiritual masters—principles that are timeless, rooted in compassion, forgiveness, and awareness.

Through regular meditation and sincere self-inquiry, you begin to align your life with these laws. As your awareness deepens, you become attuned to life's subtle harmonies and better equipped to respond rather than react.

The Slavery of Anger and the Path of Liberation

Unaddressed anger is like an untamed fire—it scorches everything in its path. It consumes the mind, distorts the heart, and poisons relationships. But when you pause, breathe, and observe your anger without judgment, you create the space to **transform its energy** into higher emotions like understanding, empathy, and compassion.

This is not suppression. Suppression blinds you to anger's lessons. Transformation, on the other hand, requires **tremendous willpower and self-honesty.** You must confront the ego that fuels your rage and say, "No more shall I be your slave."

The Teachings of the Masters

Jesus Taught: The Path of Forgiveness

"He who lives by the sword shall perish by the sword." This is the law of **karma** in motion: what you give, you receive.
He also said:

"Judge not, and you shall not be judged. Condemn not, and you shall not be condemned. Forgive, and you shall be forgiven."

These teachings remind us that the **path of forgiveness** is not weakness—it is **divine strength.**

G.I. Gurdjieff Shared: Awareness Dissolves Anger

The Mystic philosopher once shared a story from his childhood.

On his grandfather's deathbed, he was given this single, powerful instruction:

"Whenever you get angry, postpone your decision by 24 hours."

This one simple act became a spiritual practice that helped Gurdjieff rise to extraordinary inner heights. Even **pausing for a few minutes** before acting in anger can open the door to awareness—and in that space, transformation begins.

In moments of mindfulness, anger cannot survive. Anger is a **creature of unconsciousness**; it thrives in the shadows. But when you bring the light of awareness to your thoughts and emotions, anger begins to dissolve.

Let anger become your **wake-up bell.** When it flares, don't rush to react. Instead, take it as a signal: "Something in me needs attention." In this way, anger serves a purpose—it alerts you to unconscious habits, wounds, or imbalances that are asking for healing.

Buddha Said: What Is the Path of Peace

"Those who are free of resentful thoughts surely find peace."

Anger and resentment cloud the mind. Let your inner world be like a still lake, not a stormy sea. Clear it daily. Release emotional clutter as you would take out the garbage. A **clean mind** is a happy mind.

Baba Lokenath Taught: Mental Cleansing

The great Himalayan sage **Baba Lokenath** gave a beautiful and practical practice for mental cleansing. Each night before sleep, reflect on your day. If you find yourself holding anger or resentment toward anyone, bring that person's image into your mind. Gently release any ill feelings. Forgive. Let go.

Repeat this practice regularly. Over time, the **power of anger fades**, replaced by love, clarity, and lightness of heart.

Thakur Bhajan Brahmachari Instructed: Use Words Wisely
"The time you take to say a few kind and healing words is the same time you take to utter words that hurt and humiliate another. Why waste your breath creating bad karma through anger and cruelty? Don't forget—whatever you give out today, you will receive in return, sooner or later!"

This profound reminder calls us to **conscious speech.** Words spoken in anger can leave wounds deeper than any weapon. But a word of kindness can uplift a soul.

The Soul's True Nature is Love

Anger and resentment are **not the qualities of your soul.** They are products of a reactive mind, born of hurt, fear, and ego. What is born must die—and so must anger. But your **true essence**—love, compassion, and forgiveness—is eternal. These are the sacred qualities of the soul.

By aligning with these divine traits, you do more than transform your own life—you become a vessel through which peace, light, and harmony flow into the world. In a world fragmented by division, anger, and fear, your **inner peace** becomes a radical act of healing.

Conclusion: The Eternal Fire of Love

Let the teachings of the great spiritual masters be your compass. Let anger become your teacher, not your tyrant. Walk the path of awareness, forgiveness, and divine remembrance.

And when the fire of anger rises within you, use it—not to destroy—but to **illuminate the path to your higher self.**

As you evolve, the energy of anger will no longer be a force of destruction. It will become a **flame of transformation,** leading you from ego to essence, from reaction to realization, from resentment to radiant love.

CHAPTER 5

RESEARCH ON NEUROLOGICAL AND SPIRITUAL PERSPECTIVES OF ANGER

Q#5: What Is the Research on Neurological and Spiritual Perspectives on Anger?

Anger is a deeply human emotion—neither inherently good nor bad, but a **signal.** Modern science and ancient spiritual wisdom both affirm that anger is not something to fear or suppress, but something to **understand, observe, and eventually transform.** Rather than being separate, the neurological and spiritual perspectives on anger complement and enrich each other.

Let's explore the intersection of these two powerful lenses:

1. Anger as an Instinct

From a neurological standpoint, anger originates as a **survival**

mechanism. When faced with a perceived threat, the brain activates the **fight, flight, or freeze** response through the amygdala, releasing a cascade of stress hormones. This immediate reaction is designed to protect us.

However, in modern life, the threats we face are more psychological than physical—insults, injustice, stress, or rejection. Our bodies still react as if the threat were physical, but the **energy of anger**, rather than being used and released, often lingers and festers, causing long-term harm to body, mind, and relationships.

According to psychologist **Richard Lazarus**, our emotional responses are not purely instinctual or automatic. Instead, they stem from how we *evaluate* a situation. This is known as **Cognitive Appraisal**—our perception shapes our emotional response. In other words, it's not *what happens* that determines how you feel—it's *how you think about what happens.*

According to **Cognitive Behavior Therapy**, a situation unfolds, and our thoughts about it generate feelings, leading to behaviors that influence the situation positively or negatively. This cyclical process repeats, emphasizing the interconnectedness of thoughts, emotions, behaviors, and their impact on ongoing situations. In other words, thoughts influence emotions, leading to actions that, in turn, affect thoughts, creating emotions in a continuous cycle. This cycle will persist without intervention to disrupt the pattern.

Spiritual teachings remind us that **the moment the external threat is gone**, the emotion should dissolve. If it doesn't, it means the **mind has become attached** to the memory or story, feeding the flame of anger long after the fire was needed.

2. Healthy Anger as an Intelligent Response

Both science and spiritual teachings agree: **anger, when healthy and conscious, is a gift.** It alerts us when boundaries are crossed. It helps us stand up for justice, truth, and self-respect.

Healthy anger is not reactive; it is **responsive.** It arises, speaks its truth clearly, and then subsides. It doesn't leave behind a toxic residue of guilt, blame, or hate.

Dr. Gabor Maté, a renowned trauma expert, explains that **healthy anger is vital**, especially when boundaries are violated. But when anger is suppressed, it morphs into passive-aggressive behavior, depression, or chronic illness. Spiritual traditions echo this wisdom: **suppressed anger poisons the heart**, while expressed mindfully, it purifies and protects.

3. The Influence of Modern Life on Anger

In today's hyperconnected, overstimulated world, the triggers for anger are relentless. Social media, 24/7 news, competitive work environments, and rising economic and emotional stress have all contributed to an epidemic of chronic irritation and rage.

- **Stress during pregnancy** has even been shown to affect a child's future emotional regulation. The NIH reports that **prenatal stress** can imprint emotional patterns in the unborn child, influencing their sensitivity to anger and aggression throughout life.

- **Toxic parenting**, rooted in unresolved generational trauma, often leads to emotional neglect, creating adults who don't know how to process emotions like anger constructively.

Psychologist **Dr. Jonice Webb** emphasizes that **emotional neglect**—the absence of attuned parental attention to emotions—is just as damaging as overt abuse. It silently shapes a child's emotional blueprint, making healthy anger expressions seem either forbidden or foreign.

4. Rewiring the Brain: The Role of Mindfulness and Meditation

Thankfully, neuroscience offers hope through the concept of **neuroplasticity**—the brain's ability to rewire itself. Practices like **mindfulness, meditation, deep breathing, mantra repetition (Japa), and gratitude journaling** activate brain regions associated with **empathy, compassion, and emotional regulation.**

Neuroanatomist **Dr. Jill Bolte Taylor** introduces the **"90-second rule"**:

When we react emotionally, the brain's chemical response lasts only **90 seconds.** If anger persists beyond that, it's because we've chosen to **replay the story** in our minds.

This insight aligns beautifully with spiritual teachings that urge us to **pause**, to watch the wave of emotion rise and fall without attachment. In that pause lies power—the power to choose a new response.

5. Energy Transformation: The Spiritual View

From the yogic and Vedantic perspective, **anger is energy (shakti)**—a force that can be transformed rather than suppressed. Energy is never destroyed, only redirected. If you suppress anger, it turns inward, manifesting as anxiety, depression, or physical disease. But if you bring **awareness** to it, you can transmute it into **compassion, courage, or creative force.**

Spiritual teacher **Tara Brach** encourages the use of the **RAIN method:**

- **Recognize** the emotion
- **Allow** it to be there without judgment
- **Investigate** the unmet need beneath it
- **Nurture** the part of you that is hurt or afraid

This method reflects the essence of spiritual practice: turning toward suffering with kindness, not resistance.

6. Anger and the Soul's Evolution

Ultimately, spiritual traditions teach that anger is a **milestone on the soul's journey.** Every time you pause instead of reacting, **you move closer to your true Self.** Anger then becomes a guidepost, a flare showing where more love, clarity, or boundaries are needed.

You begin to see that those who provoke you are **unconscious actors in your play,** giving you a chance to grow in patience and strength. This doesn't mean you accept abuse or stay silent—it means you act from your **center,** not from your wounds.

7. The Union of Science and Spirituality

Science explains the *how*—how the brain works, how patterns form, how chemicals flood the system.

Spirituality explains the *why*—why we suffer, why we repeat patterns, and how to transcend them.

Together, they offer a complete roadmap:

- Science shows that **anger is biological** but can be transformed through neuroplasticity.
- Spirituality teaches that **anger is energetic** and can be alchemized into love through mindfulness and compassion.

This synthesis empowers us to embrace our anger—not with fear, but with wisdom.

8. Emotional Brain Training: Rewiring the Emotional Circuitry

Adding to the growing body of research on neuroplasticity, **Laurel Mellin**, a pioneer in emotional health and neuroplasticity, has developed a groundbreaking approach called **Emotional Brain Training (EBT).** This method is based on the understanding that our emotional responses are **not fixed traits**—they are deeply ingrained **neural circuits** that can be **rewired through intentional practice.**

EBT teaches that emotions like **anger, anxiety, shame, and frustration** are the result of overactive stress circuits. When we engage in **mindful emotional processing**, we shift the brain's operating system from a state of stress to a state of **resilience, joy, and love.**

According to Mellin, when we identify and deactivate the negative circuitry by working through emotional layers and rewiring the brain step-by-step, we don't just **manage** emotions like anger—we **transform them.** Over time, we strengthen the brain's **reward circuits**, which increases our capacity for peace, compassion, and connection.

This approach aligns beautifully with spiritual practices that emphasize:

- Witnessing your emotional states without judgment
- Redirecting energy toward compassion and higher awareness
- Retraining the subconscious mind with love-based affirmations

In this way, EBT bridges the gap between **scientific insight and spiritual wisdom**, offering practical tools for deep inner transformation.

The Takeaway: Anger Is Not the Enemy—Unconsciousness Is

Whether through the **RAIN method, EBT**, or ancient spiritual practices like **meditation, Japa, or mindfulness**, we are reminded of one truth: **we are not our anger.** Anger is a passing wave—**you are the ocean beneath it.**

When we become the observer of anger instead of the victim of it, we reclaim our power. When we pause, breathe, and choose awareness, we activate the dormant potential of the soul and the plasticity of the brain.

Let every rising tide of emotion
become a sacred invitation—
not to react, but to rise.
Not to harden, but to soften.
Not to blame, but to awaken.

HOW TO MANAGE AND APPROPRIATELY EXPRESS ANGER

CHAPTER 6

WE EMBRACE ANGER TO TRANSFORM IT

Q#6: How do I get rid of my anger?

The very fact that you are becoming aware of your anger is a significant step forward. However, don't feel guilty about having anger—it's part of the human experience. Instead of rushing to eliminate it, focus on transforming it from within. Anger is not just a flaw; it has roots in our evolutionary biology. It once served as a protective mechanism for survival, defending our boundaries and ensuring safety.

But times have changed. What we once used to guard ourselves now often harms us and those around us. Still, if you try to condemn or suppress anger, you'll find that it doesn't disappear—it gathers strength underground and can erupt as rage when you least expect it. That's why the spiritual path doesn't ask us to fight anger—it invites us to *observe it*, *understand it*, and ultimately *transmute it*.

Modern neuroscience supports this truth. Studies show that regular mindfulness and meditation enhance the areas of the brain associated with compassion and love, while reducing the neural activity that fuels anger and resentment. The brain is malleable—thanks to neuroplasticity, you can rewire how you respond to triggers over time.

Transforming Anger through Awareness

When anger begins to rise, try not to *become* it. Instead, watch it like a flame flickering in your mind. Separate yourself from the reaction. Most people who suffer from chronic anger have developed mechanical, unconscious responses to emotional triggers. But just as these reactions were formed, they can be unlearned.

Your desire to change must be *genuine*—not from fear or shame, but from a deeper longing for peace. Books and talks can inspire you, but transformation happens only when you choose to practice what you know. Awareness is the fire that purifies. Every time you observe the "smoke" of anger before it becomes a blaze—when you notice the tightening of your chest, the rush of adrenaline, the racing heartbeat—you've already won your first victory.

This pause, this sacred space between impulse and action, is where transformation happens. It may be small at first, but that moment of presence is powerful. It's the crack through which the light of self-mastery begins to enter.

The Power of Observation

Daily mindfulness—especially during moments of joy or stillness—strengthens your connection with the *Observer within*, the *Witness*. This Observer is not reactive. It is still, calm, and always present. The more you connect with this inner witness, the more easily you'll be able to do so even during emotional storms.

Observation itself is a form of meditation. Science has shown that focused awareness can change the molecular and energetic structure of what is being observed. As you watch your anger, you loosen its grip. It begins to dissolve, and in its place arises something softer—compassion, understanding, peace.

Stay Awake. Stay Rooted.

To live consciously is to live from the center of your being—not the noisy, chaotic periphery where anger and fear dwell. Humanity today is suffering not because of a lack of information, but due to a deep disconnection from the Self. We are like trees cut off from our roots, trying to survive in barren soil.

Despite our scientific achievements, one in three people in advanced societies suffers from some form of mental or physical illness. This epidemic of suffering stems from forgetting who we are: beings of love, joy, light, and stillness.

The remedy lies in *remembering*. In *returning*. Through meditation, self-inquiry, and simple acts of awareness—like watching your breath, your body, or your thoughts—you begin to reestablish the sacred connection to your true nature.

Just as you can stand by a window and watch the clouds pass without becoming the sky, you can learn to observe your emotions without becoming them. You are not your thoughts. You are not your anger. You are the awareness in which all of these arise and dissolve.

A Glimpse of Freedom

Once you glimpse this truth—that you are the Seer, not the seen—a shift begins. You realize *I am not my anger. I am not even my mind. I am something deeper, quieter, more luminous.* This is the beginning of liberation.

This is the path of real transformation—not suppression, not judgment, but sacred observation. From this space, anger loses its grip, and the wisdom of your being begins to flow.

Closing Reflection

"Just as a flame flickers and fades when not fed, so too does anger subside when not fueled by unconscious reaction. Watch it. Understand it. Transform it. Then you will no longer be a prisoner of your emotions, but a master of your Self."

Let this be your journey—from reactivity to radiance, from anger to awareness, from resistance to realization.

CHAPTER 7

DO NOT DEFINE YOURSELF AS ANGRY

Q #7: I've been such an angry person lately. Everything seems to be going wrong in my life. It's hard to see anything good anymore. Everyone around me is negative, too. I don't like this version of myself. What can I do to control these overwhelming feelings?

The first and most important step is this: **do not define yourself by your anger.** The moment you say, *"I am an angry person,"* you create a powerful self-suggestion that imprints deeply into your subconscious. Even if you feel angry often, **don't identify with it.** Don't say, *"This is just how I am,"* or *"I always lose my temper when things go wrong."* These repeated declarations become a sort of **self-hypnosis**—they program your inner mind to believe anger is a part of your identity. And what the subconscious believes, it works hard to fulfill.

Your subconscious doesn't understand irony or self-deprecation. It only hears the words *"angry," "always," "habitual"* and takes them as truth. This is how your inner wiring gets stuck in a negative loop.

Instead, begin to affirm something higher.

Say to yourself:
"I am learning to respond with calm."
"I choose compassion over reaction."
"Peace is possible, even now."

These are not just affirmations—they are seeds. With regular practice, they will grow into a new way of being.

Why We Stay Stuck in Anger

It's understandable to feel overwhelmed when nothing seems to go right and the people around you are caught in their own negativity. But anger often arises not because of external triggers—but because of how we process them internally.

When the ego feels hurt, helpless, or disappointed, it reacts. It wants to defend, resist, control. But the problem is not the emotion itself—it's the **unconscious reaction.**

Anger is like a fire. If you feed it with more anger, it spreads. But if you pause and choose to observe it—without judgment—you take away its fuel.

You are not helpless.
You are not broken.
You are not your worst emotion.

Transforming Anger Through Awareness

Let's be clear: trying to "control" anger in the moment often fails. Why? Because control implies suppression, and what you suppress festers. **Don't try to suppress anger. Transform it.**

How?

1. **Change your inner language.**
   Begin replacing self-limiting beliefs with gentle, empowering ones. Catch yourself every time you label yourself with anger or despair—and shift the story.

2. **Pause before reacting.**
   When anger begins to rise, take a deep breath. Even a five-second pause breaks the automatic chain. That pause is your power.

3. **Reflect, don't react.**
   After the moment has passed, ask yourself: "*What was I really feeling? What hurt me?*" Often, anger is a mask for pain, fear, or sadness. Identifying the root emotion brings healing.

4. **Feed compassion, not the fire.**
   The antidote to anger is not force, but **compassion**—for yourself, for others, for your situation. This may feel impossible at first, but even a small shift—saying, "*This person may be hurting too,*"—can open a new pathway.

You Are Not Alone

Many people feel just like you. The world today is heavy with fear, confusion, and noise. But just because everyone else is angry or negative doesn't mean you have to be. Your suffering is not a sign of weakness. It's a sign that your soul is awakening to something deeper.

You are being called to a higher response. To return to the peace that lives within you.

Start today with one kind thought toward yourself. One gentle breath. One moment of pause before reacting.

And remember:

You are not here to control the storm.
You are here to become still within it.

CHAPTER 8

THE THREE GUNAS: UNDERSTANDING THE LEVELS OF ANGER ACCORDING TO OUR NATURE

Q #8: If I need to have the other person understand that I am not very happy with the unexpected way they behaved, interacted, or talked with me, how do I show anger appropriately without having anger burn me up inside?

Individuals Act According to Their Natural Tendencies—The Three Gunas

The very fact that you're asking *how* to express anger reveals a growing awareness within you. This awareness is the first step on the path of transformation.

In the wisdom of the **Bhagavad Gita** and **Samkhya philosophy**, human behavior is shaped by the dynamic interplay of the **three Gunas:**

- **Sattva** (purity, harmony, wisdom)
- **Rajas** (passion, restlessness, ambition)
- **Tamas** (inertia, ignorance, darkness)

Each of us operates from a unique blend of these Gunas. And this inner composition influences how we **feel, think**, and **react**—especially in moments of emotional intensity like anger.

The Root of Anger Is Internal

Anger is not created by another person's words or actions. It is **activated** by them, but its **origin lies within.** Our upbringing, conditioning, and unconscious emotional patterns (often modeled by parents or early influences) determine how we react.

We cannot realistically aim to eliminate anger entirely. But what we **can** do is *transform* it—elevate it to a conscious expression that serves growth rather than destruction.

Understanding the Guna-Driven Responses to Anger

- **Tamas (Unconscious and Destructive Anger)**
  In this state, anger is reactive, blind, and damaging. It often leads to emotional outbursts, passive aggression, blame, or even violence. The tamasic mind is clouded—it reacts without awareness and inflicts harm both outwardly and inwardly.

- **Rajas (Impulsive, Ego-Driven Anger)**
  Here, the person is more active and assertive, but still driven by personal desire, ego, and emotional turbulence. Anger under rajas may feel justified and energetic, but it lacks the

stillness of discernment. It fuels arguments, harsh judgments, and regretful actions.

- **Sattva (Transformed, Conscious Anger)**
  Sattva brings clarity and control. In this elevated state, anger may still arise, but it no longer possesses you. You witness it with detachment, assess the situation, and respond with measured clarity. You might speak firmly, but with love. You may set a boundary, but without burning bridges. This is **anger as awareness**, not reaction. It is the gentle power of a **mother disciplining with love**, or a **teacher correcting with compassion.**

How to Express Anger Without Being Burned by It

As you progress on your spiritual path, you begin to move away from tamasic reactions and rajasic impulsiveness. You may find yourself more introspective, questioning the source of your anger, and seeking healthier ways to express dissatisfaction without hurting yourself or others.

Here are a few **practical approaches** to help you manage and **express anger appropriately:**

1. **Pause Before You React**
   Take a breath. Create space between stimulus and response. That pause is where wisdom enters. Anger thrives on immediacy—Sattva arises from stillness.

2. **Acknowledge the Feeling, But Don't Become It**
   Say to yourself: *"Anger is arising in me, but I am not anger."*
   This shifts your identity from the emotion to the observer of the emotion. From there, clarity begins.

3. **Use Firm Yet Respectful Words**
   When you need to express your displeasure, be clear and direct, but not hurtful. Say, *"I felt uncomfortable with the way that situation unfolded. I'd like us to speak about it calmly."*
   Such statements come from a balanced mind—not a reactive ego.

4. **Reflect on the Gunas at Play**
   Was your reaction tamasic, rajasic, or sattvic? Use this understanding not to judge yourself, but to **transform.** This inner inquiry is the essence of spiritual maturity.

5. **Practice Daily Self-Purification**
   Meditation, mindful breathing, prayer, and journaling help cleanse the mental field. These practices gradually reduce your emotional reactivity and bring the sattvic quality of serenity into your life.

6. **Protect Your Energy Without Building Walls**
   Sometimes, compassion means stepping away. You don't have to engage in every battle. **Withdraw with grace** when necessary and return when you are grounded in peace.

Anger Is an Opportunity for Inner Evolution

Anger is not inherently bad. When used wisely, it is a signal, a call for change, a motivator for truth. But if mishandled, it becomes a fire that scorches the very soul it seeks to protect.

You are not being asked to suppress your anger, but to **refine** it.

Transform it from fire to light. From reaction to insight.

Remember this sacred truth:

The one who can remain composed in the presence of provocation is the one who walks in the footsteps of sages.

Let your goal be not to *never feel anger*, but to *rise above it*.

As you cultivate more Sattva through awareness, devotion, and practice, anger will cease to dominate you—it will simply pass through, like a cloud drifting across the sky.

Let this be your path.

CHAPTER 9
TRANSFORMING JUDGMENT INTO INNER PEACE

Q #9: Why do I feel so guilty and stressed when I get angry and criticize someone, even if they deserve it? I've noticed others can criticize without feeling bad, but I feel like I've committed a crime. Should I stop venting when mistreated—or find a way to express myself without guilt, even though that seems impossible?

Your question reveals a sacred awareness beginning to awaken in you—the sensitivity of a heart that no longer wants to add to the suffering in the world.

Yes, many people criticize, lash out, and hurt others without batting an eye. But the fact that *you* feel pain after doing so doesn't make you weak—it's a sign of your evolving consciousness. You're not just reacting anymore; you're *watching* yourself react. That's the beginning of wisdom.

We're all on a conveyor belt of spiritual growth—a journey

of being groomed, tested, and refined by life itself. You're not meant to label others as bad and yourself as good. Instead, understand this: every soul is at a different point on the spectrum of awareness. Everyone is walking their own path, learning through trial and error. And yes, mistakes—your own and others'—are great teachers on this journey.

Why the Guilt Arises

You feel guilty because you're no longer aligned with the energy of judgment. That is no longer your vibration. You've outgrown the old habit of venting anger and are being invited into a subtler, higher way of living—one rooted in inner peace, compassion, and responsibility.

When someone mistreats you, you *can* speak your truth. But learn to do it from a place of grounded awareness rather than emotional overflow. Otherwise, after the explosion, you're left with the smoke of regret. Guilt is not punishment—it's your soul whispering, "*This is no longer who you are.*"

Why People Hurt Others Unconsciously

Many people are wounded. Some carry traumas from childhood—emotional scars that never healed. They may react with anger, control, or apathy because they don't yet know how to love, listen, or respond with maturity. Expecting enlightened behavior from those stuck in unconsciousness only sets you up for pain. Even you may have at times, mirrored their toxicity—raising your voice, reacting impulsively—only to feel the sting of self-reproach. That's because your inner compass is trying to point you back home to your true Self.

Stop the Cycle of Judgment

Criticism, when coming from a place of ego or resentment, only feeds a loop of negativity. But here's a subtle truth: *every person is right at their own level of awareness*. From their point of view, their actions make sense—even if they hurt you.

Judging others is like standing in a fog and complaining about limited vision. What's really needed is not blame—but clarity. As you evolve, so will they—each in their own time, through their own lessons.

Clear the Inner Clutter

Before you try to "set the world right," begin by tending to your own inner world. If your heart is heavy with judgment, anger, or hurt, it will reflect in your relationships and your health. As Jesus said, "*He who lives by the sword shall perish by the sword.*" What you send out returns to you—this is the sacred law of karma.

Let go of the illusion that you must correct everyone. Instead, cleanse the lens through which you see them. If someone is blind, you don't scold them—you offer help. Similarly, those lost in negativity are not your enemies—they are souls in pain. You don't need to change them. You only need to change how you *see* them.

The Miracle of Inner Transformation

Real change begins when you shift your attention from the outside to the inside—from the faults of others to the landscape of your own mind. Remove the glasses of assumption and judgment. Look again—with softness, with space, with curiosity.

When you see the good in others, even those who challenge you, something shifts. The energy you send out transforms the energy you receive. That's how inner transformation leads to outer harmony.

You don't need to suppress your feelings. You need to express them consciously—with care, honesty, and balance. Over time, as you deepen your awareness, even the need to "vent" fades. The storms settle. Peace becomes your new baseline.

Final Reflection

"Judge not, and you shall not be judged.
Condemn not, and you shall not be condemned.
Forgive, and you shall be forgiven."
—Jesus, Gospel of Luke

Your question is holy because it comes from a place of inner conflict—a signal that the ego is dissolving, and the soul is rising.

Let this be your practice:

- Speak your truth with compassion.
- Observe your reactions without judgment.
- See others not as adversaries, but as mirrors.
- And most of all, keep coming back to the quiet center within you—where peace has always lived.

Start there. The rest will follow.

CHAPTER 10

DISCOVERING OUR BEST FRIEND WITHIN: MOVING FROM BETRAYAL TO FORGIVENESS

Q#10: "My best friend betrayed me, and I'm so angry—
I can't imagine ever forgiving her.
What can I do about this situation?"

Sometimes, what we believe to be our best friend is actually a reflection of our own desires, expectations, and projections. What we call "friendship" may often be based on how someone fulfills a part of us we haven't yet fulfilled within. In truth, your *real* best friend lives inside you—your own mind, when it becomes loving, aware, self-managed, and illumined by wisdom.

When betrayal strikes, life is inviting you to look inward and uncover a more enduring truth: that the source of love, security, and peace lies not in others, but in the sanctuary of your own being. Beneath the pain, there is a treasure—*self-compassion*—waiting to be discovered. The hurt you feel is real, but it is also the gateway to deep healing, if you allow it.

From Betrayal to Awakening

All betrayals—whether real or perceived—stem from unconscious patterns. When mindfulness is absent, both you and the other person may be operating from egoic tendencies, reactivity, or unresolved pain. Misunderstandings then snowball into wounds, and wounds into broken trust.

You may feel consumed by anger, unable to forgive. But that anger, too, is part of your healing journey. Don't condemn it. Instead, become *aware* of it. Acknowledge the fire, but don't become the flame.

Healthy Anger & the Power of Mindful Response

Anger, when expressed without awareness, can destroy. But anger, when held in mindful awareness, can transform. Just as breathing happens automatically but becomes sacred when done consciously, so too can anger be experienced with presence rather than projection.

When you communicate anger mindfully, it no longer possesses you. You're not reacting—you're responding. You're drawing a boundary, not building a wall. Over time, through the cultivation of awareness, you will transcend even the *need* to get angry—because your self-worth will speak louder than your wounds.

Being kind doesn't mean being weak. Being forgiving doesn't mean tolerating mistreatment. Healthy forgiveness includes protecting your mental peace and dignity. If someone continuously hurts you, the relationship may no longer be aligned with your growth. That, too, is clarity—not cruelty.

True Forgiveness Is an Act of Inner Freedom

Forgiveness is not a performance. It's not about suppressing your pain to appear "spiritual." Suppressed anger becomes stored tension—fuel for future explosions or internal illness. True forgiveness emerges from understanding, from seeing clearly—not just the other's behavior, but your own evolving journey.

The Universe, in its divine intelligence, forgives you countless times—every day—for what you do knowingly or unknowingly. Even as you harm, judge, or ignore, life still breathes through you. That same mercy is available to be mirrored in your own heart.

"Holding onto anger is like grasping a hot coal with the intent of throwing it at someone else—you are the one who gets burned."
– Buddha

This ancient truth still applies today. Anger may feel like control, like strength—but if left unchecked, it becomes a chain around your spirit.

The Karma of Reaction

Unconscious anger generates karma. When you fail to pause and reflect, your reactions take the form of words and actions that, once released, cannot be recalled. Karma is impersonal.

It doesn't punish—it mirrors. What you send out, you receive.

Often, our refusal to forgive is fear-based: *"If I forgive, will I be hurt again? Will I seem weak?"* But forgiveness doesn't mean allowing others to cross your boundaries. It means honoring your peace more than your pain. It's a statement to the universe that *you choose freedom over fear, clarity over control, and compassion over chaos.*

The Spiritual Path to Inner Healing

Forgiveness is not something you *do*; it's something you *allow.* It flows when your inner clarity rises. When you realize that your essence can never truly be betrayed—because it is beyond the grasp of others—then no wound can reach that sacred core. That is the essence of real empowerment.

When you feel hurt, *don't run away from it.* Sit with it. Breathe into it. Let the wave pass through you—not define you. Then, as the wave recedes, you may hear a softer voice within—your own higher self—offering peace instead of vengeance, release instead of resentment.

In those moments, you'll meet your true best friend—the one who was always there, quietly waiting within you.

Final Reflection

> ***"Forgiveness is the fragrance the violet sheds on the heel that has crushed it." – Mark Twain***

Let this be your mantra:

- I allow the pain, but I do not become the pain.
- I honor my truth without denying another's humanity.
- I protect my peace, not with vengeance, but with wisdom.
- I forgive not because they deserve it—but because *I* deserve peace.

The path forward is not to forget—but to release. And in releasing, you return home to yourself.

CHAPTER 11

THE RIGHT TIME TO SHOW ANGER

Q#11: When is it Appropriate to Show Anger?

In our daily lives—whether at work, with family, or in social settings—one of the greatest challenges is expressing **anger** in a way that is **constructive,** not destructive. This is especially true within the home, where emotions run deep and patterns are well-worn. So, the essential question arises:

Can we express anger without being consumed by it?

Most of us have struggled with anger at some point—reacting impulsively, regretting our words or actions later. But there is a way to navigate anger with greater awareness and wisdom.

The Role of Awareness in Transforming Anger

As we begin to practice **meditation** and cultivate **conscious awareness,** the mind starts to refine itself. Mental clutter begins to clear, and emotional residues start to dissolve. In such a state, when anger arises, we are able to *see it clearly*—as a wave passing through the field of consciousness—not something that defines us or controls us.

You may feel the heat of anger, but it does not overtake you. You retain your center. You act with intention rather than react out of impulse.

Take, for example, a mother who raises her voice to discipline her child. She may appear angry, but inwardly she remains calm and composed. Her anger is *measured*, not *emotional*. It is not an uncontrolled eruption, but a conscious expression intended to guide. This is the **distinction between feeling anger** and **being possessed by it**—and it is crucial.

As the Himalayan Sage **Baba Lokenath** wisely said:

"Be angry, but do not become blind with anger."

The danger is not in feeling anger. The danger lies in allowing it to blind us—to possess us—turning us unconscious and reckless. When anger is unrestrained, it causes harm: not only to others, but to ourselves—mentally, emotionally, and spiritually.

Anger as a Conscious Response

To master anger, we must first bring it into **conscious awareness**. Step back. Observe it. Feel its impact on your breath, your body, your voice. In that moment of observation, *you gain power.* You can then decide what kind of response the situation truly needs.

In everyday life, there are moments when expressing anger is appropriate:

- A father may scold his child to correct harmful behavior.
- A teacher may raise their voice to protect classroom discipline.
- A friend may speak firmly to uphold personal values.

But **the key is to remain inwardly free.** Let anger become a **tool of clarity**, not a vessel of chaos. Let it serve as **guidance**, not grievance. Only then does it cease to harm your mind or your body.

Setting Boundaries Without Burning Bridges

Another constructive form of expressing anger is through **clear boundaries.** Anger often builds when personal space, values, or dignity are repeatedly violated. In such cases, it's vital to communicate limits—not out of spite, but from self-respect and care.

Spiritual growth requires protection. Think of yourself as a **young sapling.** Just as a sapling needs a fence to protect it from trampling, your evolving inner life needs boundaries. These boundaries shield you from negative energies, doubt, or dismissiveness that can weaken your resolve.

Be mindful of what and whom you allow into your mental space. Invite only that which nurtures peace and insight. Over time, your roots will deepen, and you'll become resilient, able to face storms with inner steadiness.

Sometimes, that protection means speaking your truth. You might say, calmly and respectfully:

"I'm not comfortable discussing my spiritual journey with you right now. I hope you can honor the space I need."

This is not an act of anger—it's an act of love for yourself.

Choose the Right Time, Create the Right Space

Not every issue needs to be resolved in the heat of the moment. Allow space. Let silence do its work. Later—when the energy is lighter and hearts are more open—you can revisit the issue in a calm, harmonious way.

By choosing *when* and *how* you respond, you stop forcing solutions and begin **creating conditions** for mutual respect and transformation. Others may not change immediately, but your light, your calmness, your clarity can inspire them to reflect, perhaps even open to their own inner growth.

In Summary:

- **Feel anger** without being ruled by it.
- **Express it** when necessary—but never with blindness.
- **Use it** to uphold truth and protect peace—not to hurt or punish.
- **Transform it** into awareness, clarity, and strength.

Anger can burn down or light the way.
Let yours become a flame of wisdom.

CHAPTER 12

THE MASKS OF ANGER

Q#12: When my husband gets angry, I don't recognize who he is. One moment, he's like a demon, and the next, he's back to being calm and loving. What causes this sudden personality change? Who am I really married to?

When Anger Makes Someone Unrecognizable

This question arises in many homes. Even in the most loving relationships, moments of anger can give rise to expressions so hurtful and foreign that it seems like a stranger has taken over the person we love.

In reality, you are seeing two faces of the same person—one conscious, the other unconscious.

When someone is overwhelmed with anger, they enter a state of *temporary unconsciousness*. In such a state, people say and do things they don't fully comprehend. Their tone changes, their facial expressions contort, their eyes may become wild.

It's like they're possessed. Then, once the rage has passed, they often return to their usual gentle, caring selves, leaving you confused and shaken.

This isn't multiple personalities. This is *one person, caught between two states of mind*—the conscious and the unconscious. The same thing happens in sleep, or under the influence of alcohol. When the higher awareness is clouded, the reactive subconscious takes over, and we act without self-awareness.

Why Does This Happen?

Anger is hardwired into the human brain. It evolved as a protective response to perceived threats. But in today's complex world, it's triggered not just by physical danger, but by emotional tension, stress, unmet expectations, and internal wounds.

Our minds are full of likes and dislikes—attachments and aversions. We are drawn to what pleases us and react against what disturbs us. This reaction, when left unchecked, turns into anger. And the more suppressed anger we carry, the more volatile the eruption can be.

Often, in family life, people repress their dissatisfaction until one day, it bursts out with great force. Words stored up over the years are suddenly released, damaging trust, even breaking relationships that took decades to build.

So, Who Are You Really Married To?

You are married to both—the conscious and the unconscious sides of your husband. But you must not despair. We are all a work in progress. The spiritual journey is about *integrating* these fragmented parts into a conscious whole. It is about *replacing unconscious reactions with mindful responses.*

Controlling Anger is Not the Solution

Trying to control anger is like trying to stop a tsunami with your bare hands. The more you try to fight it directly, the more it resists. That's why the key is not suppression or control—but *transformation.*

The Principle of Anti-Anger

Rather than opposing anger with force, create something within that naturally dissolves it. Ask yourself: *"If I understood what pain or stress he is going through, would I still be this angry?"* The answer often brings compassion.

And here's a secret of the heart: *you cannot feel both compassion and anger at the same time.*

When you train yourself to look deeper—beneath the behavior, beneath the rage—you begin to see the hidden sorrow, the buried fear, the unresolved pain. And when you respond with love and empathy, the energy of anger loses its grip.

But What About My Own Pain?

Your feelings are valid. Being on the receiving end of anger—especially repeated outbursts—can be deeply wounding. This is not about excusing anyone's behavior. It is about protecting your inner peace while staying rooted in truth and wisdom.

Mindfulness and meditation can help you *observe without absorbing*—to witness the storm without being swept away by it. That's your power.

When you choose love, understanding, and forgiveness—not

as a reaction but as an *intention*—you are not submitting. You are elevating. You are setting the tone for transformation in your life and your relationship.

The Path Forward

While you cannot change someone else's anger overnight, you can change how you relate to it. By practicing:

- **Japa** (repetition of a sacred name),
- **Mindfulness** (being fully present),
- **Meditation** (stilling the inner storm), and
- **Gratitude** (focusing on the light amidst shadows),

you begin to rewire the way you process your own reactions. And in time, your peace becomes a mirror, gently encouraging the other to seek their own.

In Closing

When anger arises—whether in yourself or a loved one—see it for what it is: a sign of inner imbalance. Don't meet it with fear or retaliation. Instead, offer it your compassionate awareness. That is the beginning of healing.

Sometimes, life shakes the tree so you may discover the roots. Every moment of turbulence is also a moment of choice. And when you choose to respond with consciousness, love becomes your shield, and wisdom your compass.

ANTI-ANGER TOOLS FOR YOUR PRACTICE

Self-Care, Japa, Breathing, Mindfulness, Meditation, Compassion, Gratitude

CHAPTER 13

KEEPING YOUR INSTRUMENT PROPERLY TUNED

Q #13: I mostly feel irritated, sharp, nasty, and unkind when I am tired, hungry, thirsty, or bored. How can I build better habits to support my mental and physical health?

You are not alone. Most emotional reactivity, especially anger and irritability, has roots in **neglected self-care**—both physical and emotional. Your body and mind are intricately linked. When the body is deprived of its basic needs, the mind becomes restless, irritable, and unkind—toward others and yourself. A healthy body is the foundation of all happiness in life. The Divine has entrusted you with this body as its custodian; it is now your sacred responsibility to care for it and keep it as healthy as possible.

Start With Compassionate Awareness

Before diving into specific habits, remember **mindful change begins with compassionate self-awareness.** Don't judge yourself for these patterns. Instead, observe them as signals—your body and soul gently reminding you: "I need care. I need self-love." Each time you feel triggered, pause and ask: *Have I eaten? Slept enough? Had water? Did my routine gym or yoga? Given my mind purposeful rest?*

Now let's explore **supportive habits**, grounded in both **practical wisdom** and **spiritual awareness.**

1. **Honor Your Sleep as Sacred**

   Fatigue is fertile ground for reactivity. An unrested mind cannot discern wisely; it reacts by default. Sleep is not just physical rest—it is a time when your brain detoxifies, your nervous system resets, and your subconscious mind processes emotions.

   - *Mindful Habit:* Go to bed and wake up at consistent times, ideally rising before sunrise. The early morning hours, known as **Brahma Muhurta** in Vedic wisdom, are ideal for calmness and meditation. Avoid screens before bed—blue light from phones disrupts your melatonin, the natural sleep hormone. Instead, **create a bedtime ritual:** dim lights, drink herbal tea, listen to calming chants or soft instrumental music.

   - *Spiritual Insight:* Sleep is a sacred surrender. Offer your worries to the Divine before sleeping. Say silently, "I let go of all burdens. I trust the Universe to guide me through the night and into a new day. All is well in my life, for I am eternally protected by the Divine."

2. **Eat to Nourish, Not Just to Fill**
   Hunger magnifies anger. When your blood sugar drops, your brain's survival mode activates. This reduces patience, tolerance, and kindness. Eating mindfully **prevents "hanger"** and supports emotional steadiness. Don't skip breakfast or fall into the habit of binge eating. Your health begins with what you choose to place on your tongue.

   ❖ *Mindful Habit:* Eat **at regular intervals,** with a focus on **fresh, whole foods**—fruits, vegetables, whole grains, and plant-based proteins. Minimize processed, overly spiced, or heavy foods that dull the mind and agitate the body. Eat in a calm environment, **away from screens or distractions,** and chew slowly, and chew a greater number of times mindfully, savoring each bite. This is mindful eating. A simple practice to be more mindful.

   ❖ *Spiritual Insight:* Food is **prasad,** a sacred offering. Before eating, offer gratitude silently: "*Thank you, Universe, for this nourishment.*" Your mindset while eating affects how your body digests and your mind processes emotions.

3. **Hydrate with Awareness**
   Dehydration distorts mood. Your brain is over 70% water; even mild dehydration leads to fatigue, brain fog, and irritability.

   ❖ *Mindful Habit:* Drink **pure water** regularly throughout the day. **Drink sitting down, not standing**, and sip slowly—this helps your body absorb water better and supports calm digestion. Avoid excessive caffeine or sugary drinks (white poison), which further dehydrate.

- *Spiritual Insight:* Water is a sacred purifier. As you drink, visualize negative emotions and toxins washing away. Affirm silently: *"I cleanse myself with this water; I invite health, healing, and peace into every cell."*

4. **Move Your Body to Calm the Mind**
   Stagnation fuels boredom, and boredom feeds anger. A stagnant body leads to a restless mind. **Movement is medicine.** It clears emotional congestion and stimulates the flow of *prana*, your vital energy.

   - *Mindful Habit:* Daily exercise can be simple—a walk, gentle yoga, dancing, or breath-work. Move your body in a way that feels joyful, not forced. Prioritize **morning movement** to awaken energy and evening stretches to release tension.

   - *Spiritual Insight:* Movement can be prayer in motion. As you walk or stretch, repeat affirmations or a mantra silently. Let movement reconnect you to **inner stillness.** The calmer your body, the calmer your mind.

5. **Break Free from Screen Addiction**

   - **Constant digital stimulation fragments attention** and overstimulates your nervous system. The result? Mental fatigue, short temper, shallow breathing, and reactive moods.

- *Mindful Habit:* Designate **tech-free times**, especially early morning, during meals, and before sleep. Replace passive scrolling with **active presence**—spend time in nature, with loved ones, or in solitude. Observe your breath, journal, or practice mantra.

- *Spiritual Insight:* Your mind craves silence. Every moment you spend away from screens, you return to yourself. Technology is a tool—don't let it become your master.

6. **Create Restful "Mind Breaks" During the Day**
   Boredom is not emptiness—it's a signal. It means your mind is craving purposeful stillness, not mindless distraction. Most people, when bored, reach for a screen or vent frustration. Instead, train yourself to reach for **your breath.**

   - *Mindful Habit:* Take **2-minute breath breaks** every hour. Simply pause, sit upright, and take 3 deep, slow breaths. Let go of tension with each exhale. This simple reset **prevents mental overload** and emotional snap reactions.

   - *Spiritual Insight:* Stillness is not wasted time. In stillness, the Divine whispers. Each conscious breath is a prayer, a return to peace.

Final Word: Habits Are Sacred Acts of Self-Love

To feel less sharp, irritable, or reactive, you must treat yourself as **sacred.** Your body, mind, and breath are gifts—they need mindful care, just like a temple needs cleaning and reverence.

There is **no quick fix.** But each time you choose rest over chaos, water over caffeine, a walk over scrolling, a breath over a reaction—you shift your destiny.

Your new life is built one conscious habit at a time.

In Summary:

- **Sleep regularly**—rest is sacred and resets your mind.
- **Eat mindfully**—food is medicine and a divine gift.
- **Hydrate with presence**—water cleanses body and mind.
- **Move daily**—motion dissolves stagnant emotion.
- **Unplug wisely**—a digital detox restores attention and peace.
- **Breathe often**—your breath is your sanctuary and healer.

Start small. Commit to **one habit this week.** Let it anchor you. Then add another. Over time, you'll find your irritability fading, replaced by calm presence and spontaneous kindness.

You deserve that peace—and the world around you will mirror it. In that peace, you will feel truly alive for the first time.

CHAPTER 14

THE MAGIC OF JAPA

Q #14: What can I do to stop the incessant chatter in my mind?

You are, in essence, the sum total of your repeated actions—your *practices*. Your brain learns from all that you repeatedly do, not just in this lifetime, but through countless incarnations in various forms. It's no wonder, then, that your mind feels constantly overstimulated and unable to pause—it has been trained to operate in fast-forward mode, processing vast amounts of data in microseconds.

To calm the mental chatter, you must **retrain your brain**—not to think automatically, but to think consciously, with discernment. This ability to choose is the highest human faculty: choosing what to allow and what to reject, what serves your higher truth and what does not. This is the beginning of the journey inward, toward your true home—your being.

The Power of Mantra: Transcending the Mind

In the East, especially within the Vedic tradition of *Sanatana Dharma*, **mantras** have long served as sacred tools for tuning the mind to higher vibrations. Even modern scientific studies now affirm the immense power of sound frequencies—especially Vedic chants—to shift us from the material, sense-bound world to the quantum field of expansive consciousness.

The word *mantra* comes from two Sanskrit roots: *man* (mind) and *tra* (to transcend). A mantra, therefore, is a sound that carries the power to **transcend the mind**. Through regular repetition—*Japa*—it draws the mind away from scattered thoughts and uplifts it into silence, devotion, and inner bliss.

When the mind transcends, it means it has crossed its habitual threshold and entered a sacred space where sound merges into silence—where thoughts no longer dominate, and you rest in pure awareness. This is the real ground of stillness, where the incessant chatter dissolves naturally.

How to Practice Mantra Japa

In the Vedic path, mantras are traditionally received from a *Guru*—a realized master—through a sacred process known as **initiation** (*diksha*). The Guru not only gives a mantra but also infuses it with spiritual energy, transmitting a spark of their own realization into the heart of the seeker. This is a deeply empowering moment for one's spiritual journey.

That said, if you haven't been formally initiated, you can still choose a mantra that deeply resonates with you—one that evokes peace, devotion, or a sense of inner anchoring. Just be careful not to collect too many mantras from different sources, which can scatter your focus. **Choose one** and stick to it with love and sincerity.

A Simple Daily Japa Practice:

- **Choose a time** that suits you—ideally early morning and/or evening.
- **Find a sacred space**—preferably in the northeast corner of your home (as per *Vastu*). Sit on a mat or chair with your spine erect and body relaxed.
- **Begin with body awareness.** Close your eyes. Gently scan your body from head to toe or toe to head, part by part, acknowledging and relaxing each area with gratitude.
- **Take 3–6 deep, mindful breaths,** making your exhalation slightly longer than inhalation. This clears inner space and invites calm.
- **Invoke the Divine Presence** within. Now begin to softly repeat your chosen mantra. You may chant it aloud, whisper it, or repeat it silently within. Repeating silently within is the best way. If initiated by a Guru coming from a spiritual tradition, chanting the mantra out loud is restricted. It should be kept inside as a secret treasure.
- **Focus not just on the words but on their vibration.** Feel the mantra's energy fill your being. Let it wash through your mind like a sacred wave, dissolving lower-frequency thoughts and calming your nervous system. Over time, you'll notice a subtle but unmistakable shift: the chatter will diminish, and you'll feel more grounded, peaceful, and internally spacious.

Why This Matters

A restless mind will always block your potential—spiritually, emotionally, and even materially. Calming the mind must become a **life priority.** *Japa Yoga* or *Mantra Yoga* isn't just a spiritual exercise—it is an emotional tuning fork, aligning you with the frequencies of peace, love, compassion, and divine harmony.

No one else can make this commitment for you. Just as you must eat to nourish your body, you must consciously choose to quiet your mind and uplift your soul.

Start small—just a few minutes in the morning and evening. Stay consistent. Let your mantra be a gentle companion. With time, peace will no longer be something you seek; it will be what you *are.*

And from that peace, joy, and abundance will naturally begin to flow into every area of your life.

CHAPTER 15
BREATH, THE NATURAL ANTIDOTE TO ANGER

Q#15: Is Breath Our One-Stop Solution to Anger Management?

The Mystical Power of Breath

Even the most iconic minds of our time, such as Steve Jobs, turned to the breath as a source of grounding and renewal. He once shared, "*I notice a difference from the moment I meditate. I can be stressed or tired, and I can go into meditation and it all just flows off of me. I'll come out of it refreshed and centered, and that's how I'll feel—it'll carry through the day.*"

Indeed, if we wish to carry through a demanding day with grace and balance, we must begin by tuning our **body, mind, and breath** to the rhythm of nature and the universe. Morning practices such as **yoga, pranayama**, and **meditation** root us in the present moment. When we are centered, we are far less vulnerable to external provocations that would otherwise trigger old subconscious patterns of stress and anger.

Breath and the Smoke of Unconsciousness

Anger, in itself, is not inherently wrong—it is a **natural defense mechanism**, an evolutionary tool. But when it becomes a habitual response to life, we become victims of our **own unfriendly minds.** The prelude to anger is always a cloud of unconsciousness. And **where consciousness shines, anger dissolves.**

Practicing **mindful breathing,** even for just a few moments a day, breaks this pattern. When we consciously shift our awareness to the breath, the mind slows down, the heart softens, and a sense of calm prevails. You cannot be angry while breathing mindfully. The two states are mutually exclusive.

Try it yourself: in a moment of tension, bring your awareness inward—away from external distractions—and focus solely on your breath. You'll notice your body and mind returning to their natural, relaxed state. This is the beginning of transformation.

Breath as the Bridge Between Two Worlds

Your **breath is sacred.** It is the thread that connects the physical with the spiritual, the individual with the universal. Breath is not just air—it is **prana**, the vital life force. It flows through you in every moment, whether you are aware of it or not. But when you become conscious of it, it becomes your most powerful ally.

Abdominal breathing—what we call "baby breathing"—is one of the most effective natural stress relievers. When you breathe deeply into your belly and smile gently to the Universe, you invite healing into your whole being. Each **inhalation** becomes an infusion of new life, and each **exhalation** becomes a release of the old—tension, judgment, pain.

This is **true alchemy.** With every breath, you are reborn.

The Science and Spirit of Breath

Scientific research has now affirmed what ancient yogis knew centuries ago: breath is the master key to regulating emotions, enhancing clarity, and restoring the body's natural balance. With just a few deep, **conscious breaths**, you can transform your thoughts, shift your emotions, and purify your inner world.

Whenever anxiety or fear arises, practice this simple shift:

Take **three deep inhalations and exhalations**, letting go naturally.

Feel your connection to the **vital force** within you.

This conscious shift moves you from reaction to response, from dis-ease to ease.

Over time, **breathwork becomes your sanctuary**—a spontaneous way of living, a path to enriched awareness and joyful presence.

Transformative Breath Practices

1. **Bhramari Pranayama (Humming Bee Breath)**

   A deceptively simple yogic technique with profound neurological and emotional effects. It soothes the brain, regulates anxiety, and calms the heart—often within seconds.

   How to do it:

   - Close your ears gently with your thumbs.

- Cover your eyes lightly with the remaining fingers.
- Take a deep breath in, and as you exhale, hum like a bee.
- Repeat for **3 to 10 cycles.**

It is especially helpful during moments of panic, before exams, or during emotional overwhelm. Neuroscientists continue to marvel at the balancing effects it brings to the **autonomic nervous system.**

2. **Nadi Shodhana (Alternate Nostril Breathing)**
   This is the **breath of balance**, harmonizing the body, mind, and spirit. It realigns the **left and right hemispheres of the brain**, marrying logic with intuition, action with rest.

   How to do it:
   - Gently close your **right nostril** with your thumb.
   - Inhale through the **left nostril**, pause.
   - Release the right nostril and **exhale slowly** through it.
   - Now inhale through the **right nostril**, pause.
   - Exhale through the **left nostril.** This completes one cycle.
   - Repeat for **3 to 10 cycles.**

This practice not only supports **physical immunity** and **respiratory health** but also awakens your **subtle body**, allowing you to vibrate in tune with the universal rhythm of life.

Final Reflection: Breathe, and Be Free

You do not need to escape life to be at peace.
You only need to breathe consciously—to return to yourself.

Breath is your one-stop solution, not just for anger, but for all forms of mental and emotional dis-ease. Each breath is a silent teacher, a gentle healer, a constant companion.

The breath does not judge. It does not hold on to the past. It simply **flows**, inviting you into the present moment.

So, love your breath. Cherish it. Return to it again and again.

For within your breath lies the blueprint of **happiness, health, love, and peace**—waiting to be discovered, one mindful moment at a time.

CHAPTER 16

LIVING MINDFULLY AND SOULFULLY

Q#16: As a practice of mindfulness, you often emphasize the need for non-judgmental awareness to avoid self-criticism. However, we sometimes feel compelled to express our thoughts to others—often negatively and hurtfully. How can we stop this unpleasant pattern?

Mindfulness is the simple, yet profound, practice of becoming conscious of what you are doing, thinking, and feeling—moment to moment. As you develop this awareness, you begin to access the deeper layers of your unconscious mind, where habitual patterns dwell. These patterns often drive your reactions, especially the urge to speak impulsively or criticize others.

Through **mindful observation** of your thoughts, words, and actions, your mind gradually distills. You begin to notice the gaps between impulse and expression. This clarity is the foundation of personal transformation.

When you act unconsciously—on autopilot—you repeat familiar behaviors without awareness. This leads to stagnation, boredom, stress, and ultimately emotional or physical disharmony. It's a common affliction of modern life.

To break this cycle, you must *wake up* to your own life. Choose to live **mindfully and soulfully.** Let your practice take you inward, to your inner sanctum—the sacred space within your heart. Here, beneath the noise of the mind, lies your **true self:** silent, spacious, and eternal. Your body and mind change constantly, but your essence remains unshaken.

As mindfulness deepens, you begin to connect with this higher self, which is always at peace. In this space, forgiveness becomes natural. Compassion arises effortlessly. Provocations lose their power to ignite anger because you are no longer reacting from ego but responding from awareness.

The Role of Non-Judgmental Observation

Every time you observe your thoughts without judging them, you awaken your **witnessing consciousness**—the inner light that simply sees. This light purifies the mental clutter, dissolves emotional toxins, and makes room for peace, love, and joy.

With practice, you'll find that the compulsion to point out others' faults diminishes. Your speech becomes measured, your responses thoughtful. You begin to see the struggles of others—their wounds, their history, their conditioning. This insight fosters empathy. You no longer feel the need to defend your ego by diminishing others. You stop hurting others because you are no longer hurting inside.

This shift benefits not just those around you—it protects *you* from suffering. Every time you choose silence over reaction, kindness over criticism, awareness over judgment, you reclaim your energy. You become the guardian of your own peace.

Understanding the Root of Hurt

Ask yourself: *When do I feel hurt?*

You feel hurt when your expectations are not met, when your comfort is disrupted, when your sense of control is threatened.

This is where meditation and mindfulness become your true friends. They awaken you to the truth that lasting peace lies in **being unconditional**—living from a place of inner fullness, not from constant need. The fullness that happens when the mirror of your mind is cleansed.

The more mindful you are, the less you need to express your emotions reactively. Mindfulness brings purification. It dissolves toxic patterns and replaces them with understanding. Gradually, your mind stops offering hostile suggestions. Instead, it inclines naturally toward compassion and love.

This is not just wishful thinking—it is a **real transformation**, possible through sincere and consistent practice. As you grow in this awareness, your communication also transforms. You begin to embody **mindful speech**, which is not only gentle and wise, but also a vital social skill and the essence of natural leadership.

Rising Beyond Ego

There is **abundant peace** in the shrine of your own heart. As the chatter of the mind quiets, a deep contentment arises—a joy not dependent on external validation. You no longer feel the need to assert yourself, to prove anything, to be "right." If someone criticizes you, remember that many have also praised you. Which one is the truth?

Neither.

Praise and criticism are two sides of the same coin. Both come, both go. You are neither the compliment nor the insult. You are the *witness*, untouched by either.

The Final Evolution

This is the **spiritual transformation** you were born to experience. If you accept praise, be prepared to accept insult. But as you rise in awareness, you transcend this polarity altogether. You no longer live at the mercy of others' words or moods.

Instead, you abide in peace—not the peace that comes from silence outside, but from silence **within.**

I wish you a joyful journey to the realm of peace.
And always remember:
Peace is not something you seek.
It is what you become when you are fully here.

CHAPTER 17

MEDITATION, RETURNING TO STILLNESS

Q #17: Does meditation really work? I've tried to meditate to calm my anger, but I can't stop my thoughts, and I just get angrier and angrier! Meditation is making my anger worse!

You're not alone in feeling this way at the beginning of your meditation journey. Many people face similar frustration, especially when they come to meditation with the intention of quickly calming down or stopping thoughts. But meditation is not about suppression or control. It's not a tool to instantly "fix" your anger. It is a gradual return to your natural state—a harmonious flow of body, mind, and spirit aligned with the rhythm of the universe.

At first, meditation is often approached with a results-oriented mindset: "*I must calm down. I must stop my thoughts. I must feel peaceful.*" But this very approach creates inner tension and disappointment when things don't go as expected. We become impatient and judge ourselves. Meditation becomes one more thing to feel angry or inadequate about.

But here's the truth: meditation is not about doing—it's about **being.**

Anger and other emotional disturbances are not problems to be eliminated instantly. They are symptoms of deeper unrest—of a reactive mind, of unmet needs, of accumulated stress. When the inner terrain is unsettled, even small triggers from the outside world can set off intense reactions. That's why the real answer lies not in avoiding emotions, but in creating a more tranquil inner ground where those emotions no longer take root.

Meditation gently helps you create that ground. It reorganizes your brain's neural pathways and emotional patterns. Over time, it builds your resilience, softens your reactivity, and restores inner balance.

So how do you start meditating in a way that actually helps?

Begin with a simple shift: let go of expectations. Let your practice be an offering, not a demand.

- **Find a comfortable position.** Sit or lie down in a relaxed posture. Let your body feel safe and supported.
- **Close your eyes and begin to scan your body.** Bring awareness to each part, slowly inviting it to relax. Feel the tension melting.
- **Now, turn your attention to your breath.** Don't force or change it—just observe it. Inhale and exhale as naturally

as the ocean waves. Let your breath carry you like a surfer riding those waves.

- **As you inhale, say silently:** *"I breathe in peace and light."*
- **As you exhale:** *"I release anger and tension."*
- **Smile gently** and trust this silent exchange with the universe.

There is no need to control your thoughts. Let them come and go like clouds passing through the sky. Watch them without reacting. You are not your thoughts—you are the sky that holds them.

Meditation is not about time—it's about presence. Even **5 or 10 minutes a day** can shift your entire inner landscape if done with sincerity and non-judgmental awareness.

Over time, you'll notice subtle but profound changes:

- You won't get as easily provoked.
- You'll find yourself pausing before reacting.
- Your anger will lose its sharpness, its grip.
- Peace will no longer be something you seek—it will become the space you live from.

And most beautifully, love and compassion won't be something you try to practice—they will arise effortlessly as the fragrance of your blossoming Self.

Let go of the pressure to meditate "right." Just show up, day after day, with gentleness and willingness. Meditation is not about stopping thoughts; it's about **returning to stillness** despite them. The miracle happens when you stop chasing results and start trusting the process.

Be patient with yourself. This is the sacred journey of coming home—to your calm, clear, radiant Self.

CHAPTER 18

COMPASSION IN ACTION

Q #18: I was blessed to hear you speak about compassion as a way to heal this troubled world. You said that by embracing understanding, kindness, forgiveness, and love—rather than anger—we move beyond reaction into conscious living. Can you offer practical ways to live this truth daily?

Absolutely. The first step is to understand this powerful truth: It's All Energy!

Anger is energy. But so are *compassion, love, understanding,* and *forgiveness.*

We often try to push anger away. But instead of chasing it out, invite *compassion* to take root. It's already in your heart—yearning to be expressed. The more space you give to compassion, the less oxygen anger will have to survive.

Where once you said, "*I don't want to be angry, but I still get angry,*" now let your self-talk change:

"I choose to nourish love and compassion within me."

Avoid negative self-suggestions. Don't self-limit, self-condemn, or self-belittle. These become unconscious curses we place upon ourselves. The truth is, **no one curses you more than you curse yourself through inner judgment.**

You suffer not because of others, but because of these *self-imposed limitations.* Surround yourself with positive energy, thoughts, and beliefs. When you are immersed in positivity, how can anger find room to thrive?

Redefine Success: What Are You Really Striving For?

Ask yourself honestly:

Do I want to be in favor of myself—or against myself?

If you want to live in your own favor, stop seeking approval from others. Instead, begin with your *inner dialogue.* There's a constant battle of beliefs inside you. *Stabilize this first.*

Look at those who live with **true success**—not just in material wealth, but in **compassion, humility, wisdom, devotion, and surrender.** These are the *real parameters of success.* But the modern world has confused success with fame, dominance, and accumulation.

Many we idolize today are "successful" only outwardly. They sell us false values that distract us from our soul's journey. True icons are those who've passed through darkness and emerged into light—people of depth, stillness, and love. *Meeting such beings ignites your inner fire.*

Some souls walk through life joyfully, no matter their conditions. They say,

"I love God. God loves me. I am happy as I am."

Even if you don't believe in God, believe in **goodness, kind action, compassion, and inner truth.**

Do something—however small—with sincerity. It will bring peace and lasting joy.

Practice Compassion Daily

Turn compassion into a lifestyle. Choose daily acts of kindness—toward family, friends, strangers, and even those who may not be kind to you.

- Smile from the heart.
- Offer a kind word.
- Listen deeply.
- Help someone without expecting anything in return.
- Forgive those who've hurt you.
- Apologize when needed—*true humility weakens the ego and prevents conflict.*
- Say, "*I love compassion,*" until it becomes a living truth within you.

Be a conduit of divine light. Let love speak through you. Let joy rise through your actions.

When you focus on compassion and forgiveness—the opposites of anger—you naturally disarm the triggers of rage. You shift from reaction to **response**, from emotion to **elevation.**

Protect Your Heart. Honor Every Heart.

If you truly wish to be happy and spiritually fulfilled, make this a golden rule:

Do not cause pain to any heart.

Why? Because the *essence of the universe* resides in every heart. Hurt another's heart, and you hurt your own connection to the Divine.

Be a **devotee of light and love.** Everything else will find its proper place.

Let your regrets be transformed into joy. Let your pain be turned into purpose.

This is the essence of the *enlightened state.*

You Are Light and Love

Love is the very essence of who you are—not just a fleeting emotion, but the *core of your being.*

You are not merely a body of flesh and blood.

You are a spiritual being of light and love.

The more attention you give to your **inner world**—to your thoughts, your feelings, your emotions—the more transformation you invite. Conscious observation itself begins to rewire you from within.

That is where true change begins.

In Closing

Compassion in action is not a concept—it's a **daily practice**, a way of life.

By anchoring yourself in compassion:

- You elevate your inner world.
- You bring harmony to your relationships.
- You become a quiet blessing to the world.

So, walk gently. Live truthfully. Love freely.
And remember:
"Even a small act of kindness can ripple through eternity."
Let compassion become your nature.
Let love lead the way.

CHAPTER 19

GRATITUDE: THE LANGUAGE OF THE SOUL

Q #19: Why Is Gratitude the Most Powerful Antidote to Anger?

If anger is the voice of an unsettled ego, then gratitude is the song of a peaceful soul. While anger binds us to what we lack, gratitude frees us to see what we already have. It lifts the mind from its habitual ruts—fear, resentment, dissatisfaction—and tunes it to the language of the Universe, which is grace.

Gratitude is not just a feeling; it is a way of being. It is the soul's natural state—quiet, humble, and content. When you live in gratitude, you are no longer at war with yourself or the world. You see life not as something to conquer, but as a gift to be received with reverence. Each moment becomes a miracle. Each breath becomes a blessing.

In gratitude, anger cannot take root. Gratitude turns your attention from the outer to the inner, from what's wrong to what's right, from reaction to reflection. It expands the heart, softens the mind, and draws you closer to your true Self—the source of lasting peace and joy.

Gratitude is the alchemy that transforms ordinary life into sacred life. The more you give thanks, the more reasons you find to be thankful. And in this practice, your entire inner world begins to shift. Old patterns of irritation, blame, and judgment start to dissolve. Your eyes open to the beauty of simple things: a kind word, a quiet moment, a morning breeze.

A soul-centered life begins and ends with gratitude. As you give thanks for all that you are and all that you have—both the pleasant and the painful—you align yourself with the intelligence of the Universe. You no longer resist what is, but flow with it, trusting that everything is unfolding for your highest good.

Let your heart whisper "thank you" often—thank you for this life, for this breath, for this moment. Gratitude is the key that opens the gate to the present. It is the bridge between you and the divine. Walk that bridge, and you will know peace. Live in gratitude, and you will help uplift not only yourself but the collective soul of humanity.

Let us then live in gratitude—not as a fleeting practice, but as a way of life. For in gratitude, the soul finds its true home.

CREATING A PEACEFUL SOCIETY OF ONENESS

CHAPTER 20

SOME TRIED AND TRUE PRACTICES FOR ANGER

Q#20 What Are Some Tried and True Practices for Helping Us Deal with Our Anger?

Break the Pattern of Old Habits

Most of the suffering we experience today doesn't stem from the world outside but from the **mechanical habits** and inner patterns we've unknowingly nurtured over the years. These ingrained ways of thinking and reacting, often shaped by unresolved trauma or emotional conditioning, become default responses to stress, conflict, or discomfort.

True freedom begins when we become aware of these patterns and **break their unconscious hold** on us. This is not about battling the outer world—it's about **growing your mind**, cultivating your inner strength, and learning to remain anchored in your calm, witnessing self even amid chaos.

This shift doesn't happen through force or guilt but through **love for yourself**—a love that naturally births discipline, peace, and inner harmony.

Practice Self-Discipline from Love, Not Force

Everyone longs for a happy, peaceful, and healthy mind. But life often delivers contradictions. Your external world may not match your expectations, and this gap can trigger **frustration, resentment, and anger.** The larger the gap, the more intense the inner reaction.

Suppressing this anger only builds pressure. Eventually, it erupts, often in unexpected ways, and you're left confused or ashamed. That's why suppression is not the answer. Instead, seek to **transform** this negative energy into something life-giving.

This transformation becomes possible when you dedicate time each day to **turn inward**—through meditation, prayer, breathwork, or mindful silence. Even five minutes of presence can create space within the mind to observe, to pause, and to choose differently.

Feed the Subconscious with Positive Self-Suggestions

Your subconscious is always listening. You can shape it not with judgment, but with **kind, truthful affirmations.** During your quiet practice, say to yourself:

"I am a being of compassion and calm. I understand others because I understand myself."

"Those who hurt me are themselves hurting. I choose to respond with empathy, not anger."

"Even those who wrong me are souls on their own journey. May I meet them from my center, not my wound."

This isn't denial. It's **spiritual realism**—recognizing that another's harsh behavior reflects their own inner turbulence. When you are rooted in your higher self, you no longer feel the need to mirror that turbulence. You reflect light, not shadow.

Love and Compassion Are Your True Dharma

The **dharma of your soul** is not retaliation—it is compassion, clarity, and peaceful strength. When someone acts with ignorance or cruelty, it's easy to lash back. But does it bring peace? Does it heal?

Anger cannot heal anger. Fire cannot extinguish fire. When you choose **love over reaction**, you not only uplift yourself—you change the very vibration of the space around you.

You don't need to suppress your anger. Just **meet it with awareness.** Say to it:

"Ah, here you are again, old friend. I see you. But I choose differently now."

This act of choosing—of **not reacting from old programming**—is how you begin to shift your life, one moment at a time.

Act Without Being Possessed by Anger

There may be moments when expressing anger is necessary. But even then, let it be **mindful anger**—not reactive, not explosive, but channeled with awareness. Like an actor playing an angry role on stage, you deliver the emotion **without becoming it.**

This kind of controlled expression comes from deep practice. It allows you to assert boundaries, speak truth, or protect others, **without losing your inner peace.** Over time, this approach rewires your brain and emotions.

Just as a tree bends with the wind but does not break, you learn to feel emotions without being uprooted by them.

Seek the Center of Your Being

At your core lies a vast, silent reservoir of **peace, compassion, and clarity.** This is your divine inheritance—not something you must earn, but something you must remember.

Yet in daily life, we get lost on the periphery—caught in thoughts, judgments, moods, and expectations. These are not the real "you." They are like weather patterns passing through the sky of your awareness. The key is to **return to the center**, again and again.

Meditate Not to Escape, but to Return

Meditation is not about fixing something broken—it's about **returning to wholeness.** Do not approach it with pressure or high expectations. Just sit with yourself. Observe. Be still.

Let your breath be your anchor. Let your awareness be your compass.

There's no rush, no timeline. Results will come—not when you force them, but when you trust the process.

Accept Anger as a Messenger, Not an Enemy

Anger is not your enemy. It's a part of you that needs your attention—not rejection. Like a child throwing a tantrum, anger seeks your understanding. When you observe it, accept it, and love it into transformation, it **loses its control over you.**

As you stop feeding the anger, you reclaim your power.

Live the Wisdom of the Sages

No one else can manage your mind. Just as no one can digest your food for you, no one can meditate for you. You must **live the teachings**. Wisdom is not information—it is application.

But you are not alone. Every small step in awareness, every breath taken mindfully, every time you choose compassion over reaction—**you align with the saints and sages who walked this path before you.**

Your Outer World Mirrors Your Inner World

If you long for a peaceful, loving world—**become that world** within.

If everything outside feels chaotic, use it as a mirror. Ask, "*Where in me is there confusion? What thoughts, beliefs, or wounds am I still carrying?*"

As you purify your inner space, the external world begins to shift. You attract new people, new circumstances, new light.

Real change begins not with protest, but with **presence**.

Not with rage, but with **remembrance**—of who you truly are.

You are not here to react to the world. You are here to radiate the calm that heals!

CHAPTER 21
THE ART OF MINDFUL RELATIONSHIPS

Q#21: How Do We Foster More Mindful, Positive Relationships?

The Art of Mindful Relationships

The future of humanity rests not in technological breakthroughs or material advancements, but in our ability to nurture mindful, compassionate, and balanced relationships. As our outer lives grow more sophisticated, our inner lives often shrink—disconnected from the heart of what makes us truly human: love, empathy, and presence.

We live in an age of immense comfort yet growing emotional disconnection. Our electronic devices connect us instantly across continents yet often disconnect us from those sitting right beside us. We've gained speed but lost intimacy. We've built global networks yet weakened the bonds within our own families. True, we may not be able to live without technology, but **we cannot live without love.**

We Are Vibrational Beings

The root of our relational discord lies not outside but within. We are **vibrational beings**, constantly radiating energy through our thoughts, emotions, and intentions. Every word we speak, every thought we carry, contributes to the energetic atmosphere of our homes, workplaces, and communities.

If each one of us took full responsibility for the energy we bring into a space—if we chose joy, patience, forgiveness, and understanding—our collective emotional climate would shift. Our homes would heal, our relationships would bloom, and peace would become our shared reality.

The Loss of Forbearance and the Collapse of Connection

One of the quiet casualties of modern living is **forbearance**—the ability to endure, to forgive, to understand. As this virtue fades, so too do the bonds that hold families, marriages, and friendships together. Relationships crumble not because of a single flaw or conflict, but because we've forgotten how to pause, breathe, and listen without judgment.

What is the worth of all our wealth and achievements if we cannot trust, love, or live peacefully with one another?

Spirituality Begins at Home

True spirituality is not tested in temples or retreats—it is tested in the **sacred space of home.** How we manage our relationships, how we parent, how we treat our spouse or elders—these are the real markers of spiritual maturity.

It is easy to succeed in the world, to gain recognition and praise. But to maintain love, peace, and harmony in your own home—this is the real victory. Few pass through this narrow "eye of the needle."

Reaction Is Ego, Response Is Soul

Most of the pain we experience in relationships stems from our reactive nature. A **frustrated mind** lashes out, judges, and blames. But a **mindful heart** listens, reflects, and responds. Every time we react unconsciously, we deepen the discord. But every time we pause and breathe mindfully, we open space for healing.

Just as an arrow, once released, cannot be recalled, **our words—especially in moments of anger—leave lasting imprints.** Thoughtless communication is one of the greatest sources of relational suffering. We must train ourselves to speak only what we would be willing to hear, and to listen with the intent to understand, not to judge.

The Power of Meditation and Inner Calm

The **foundation of mindful relationships** is a calm mind. Meditation, reflection, and silent self-observation are not luxuries—they are necessities in a world full of noise and reactivity.

A calm mind becomes a vessel for empathy. It allows us to absorb the limitations of others with grace. It makes space for understanding and transforms hurt into healing. Those who cultivate inner peace know that a single, mindful breath can prevent a thousand storms.

Gratitude as a Sacred Practice

If you want to heal your relationships, start by expressing **gratitude.** Appreciate the small kindnesses. Acknowledge the efforts. Speak words that uplift. Gratitude is a prayer that needs no religion—it's the universal language of love.

Focus less on others' faults and more on their goodness. When you look for beauty in others, you awaken it in yourself. Your mind becomes the sacred altar where love is worshipped.

The Mirror of the Inner Home

When the **home of your mind** is clean and harmonious, your outer world follows. A disordered inner life projects confusion outward. But when your thoughts are aligned with peace and compassion, your relationships become mirrors of that inner serenity.

The **art of mindful relationships** is not about perfection. It's about **living and loving without regrets.** It is the daily decision to speak with care, to love with presence, and to forgive with sincerity.

In Summary:

- **Mindful living** is the heart of meaningful relationships.
- **You are the energy** you bring into your relationships.
- **Practice forbearance** and patience—these are divine strengths.
- **Let your home be your spiritual temple**—where your true nature is tested and revealed.

- **Respond, don't react**—and let your soul lead your communication.
- **Gratitude is your daily prayer**—let it heal what judgment cannot.
- **Create peace within**—and the world around you will begin to reflect it.

Let us, then, choose the path of mindfulness, not just in solitude but in our relationships—where it matters most. Let us become **vessels of kindness, bridges of understanding**, and living prayers of love in action.

CHAPTER 22

POSITIVE PARENTING

Q#22: If Unhealthy Anger Is Caused by Childhood Trauma, Is There a Better Way to Parent?

The Path of Conscious Parenting

Anger, when rooted in unresolved childhood trauma, often finds expression in the very relationships we hold dearest—especially in parenting. If we want to break this cycle, we must ask: Is there a better, wiser way to raise our children?

The answer lies not in complex strategies, but in the simple, yet profound principle: **Parent by Example.**

Fewer Words, More Presence

Children do not learn through lectures—they learn through observation. A child will not remember your advice as much as they will absorb your behavior. If your eyes are glued to a screen, your child will learn distraction. If your words are kind but your tone sharp, your child will feel the dissonance. But if you model calmness, presence, and mindfulness, your child will begin to internalize those very qualities.

Be the example of what you hope your child becomes. Teach mindfulness not by instruction, but by living it.

From Power to Presence

The world has changed, and with it, parenting must evolve. What today's children need is not authoritarian control, but conscious presence. We no longer live in extended joint families where values were passed down through shared stories and intergenerational bonding. Most children today grow up in nuclear homes, surrounded by screens more than siblings.

Conscious parenting means releasing the outdated mold of command-and-control. It is not about "fixing" children, but about understanding them. It is not about power, but about partnership.

Parenting without Preconceptions

Every child enters this world with their own soul blueprint. They are not blank slates, but beings on a journey. Just as you learned through your mistakes, your child, too, must walk their path. Your role is not to prevent suffering but to provide a safe and loving space where resilience, empathy, and character can be born—even through challenges.

Let your guidance be gentle, rooted in friendship, not control. Speak from the heart, not from authority. Share your wisdom without demanding it be followed. Let your words be offerings, not orders.

Turn Inward First

The heart of good parenting is not in focusing on your child, but on your **own inner life.** A tree bears sweet fruits only if its roots are deep and nourished. Likewise, children thrive in the presence of calm, centered, spiritually grounded parents.

Work first on your own inner peace. Heal your own childhood wounds. Meditate. Reflect. Breathe. From that inner stillness, you will begin to see your child not as a problem to be fixed, but as a soul to be understood.

The Illusion of Control

Modern parents often feel a need to be involved in every aspect of their child's life. But involvement can easily turn into interference. The more you try to micromanage, the more your child resists. What they seek is **freedom with guidance**, not freedom from it. Trust that the Universe is also parenting your child in unseen ways. Your faith, more than your fear, becomes the guiding light.

The Power of Friendship and Appreciation

If you want to be heard, begin by seeing the good. Appreciate your child's strengths. Speak about their virtues. This creates safety, which is the doorway to friendship. And friendship is the only soil in which trust grows.

When children trust you, they share with you. And when they share, parenting becomes effortless. You no longer need to force or insist. You simply offer your insight, and they receive it—not out of obedience, but out of mutual respect.

Speak Without Expectation

Parenting becomes peaceful when you let go of expectation. Say what you must but release the outcome. Don't speak to control; speak to connect. Don't expect immediate change, trust in slow transformation.

Your words are seeds. Some will sprout today, some in time. Say them with sincerity, not strategy.

Detachment and Spiritual Anchoring

The spiritual parent is not one who is perfect—but one who is anchored. Anchored in peace, in patience, and in faith. Parenting is a long journey, not a short campaign. Detachment does not mean disinterest—it means working from a space of love without fear, presence without pressure.

When you let go of trying to shape your child and focus on refining your own inner self, something miraculous happens: your child starts to change too. Not because you forced them—but because your energy created a safe space for them to grow.

In Summary:

- Children learn through observation—be the example.
- Shift from control to connection; from power to presence.
- Parent from your spiritual center, not your emotional reactions.
- Honor your child's soul path, not your projections.
- Let appreciation lead to friendship, and friendship to influence.
- Speak from your heart and release all expectations.

- Stay anchored in your own peace—and transformation will follow.

Let us not try to mold our children into our image. Let us become the image they naturally want to reflect. Let us become the peace we wish for them. In doing so, we may just break the generational cycle—and raise a new world through our children.

CHAPTER 23

TRANSFORMING ANGER INTO PURPOSE

Q #23: Can We Use Anger in a Positive Way?

Transforming Anger into Purpose

Anger, often feared and misunderstood, holds a hidden power. When channeled with awareness, it can become a powerful catalyst for positive change. It can fuel your courage to confront injustice, defend your boundaries, or initiate long-overdue transformation in your life. But to use anger wisely, you must understand it—not as a destructive force, but as a **raw energy** waiting to be refined.

The key lies in expressing anger **consciously**, without harming yourself or others. Anger that erupts without awareness is like fire without a container—it burns everything in its path. But anger held with mindfulness becomes a **sacred flame** that illuminates truth, ignites passion for justice, and purifies emotional stagnation.

The Role of Awareness in Anger

Anger, like any strong emotion, offers a gateway to deeper understanding—if met with awareness. In a conscious moment, anger becomes a language your inner self uses to say: "*Something needs attention.*"

When expressed mindfully, anger becomes **clarity** rather than chaos. Your tone softens, your body relaxes, and your message becomes easier for others to receive. But when expressed unconsciously, anger manifests as clenched jaws, raised voices, harsh words—revealing a mind overtaken by emotion rather than guided by wisdom.

The Prelude to Anger: Recognize the Shift

Anger never arrives without a warning. It builds quietly, often beginning with a slight disturbance in the mind—a contraction of thought, a bubbling of irritation, a subtle shift in breath or body language. Before the outburst, the **clouds gather.**

In these moments, your thoughts lose clarity, and your brain begins preparing for battle. You're no longer present; you're pulled into old emotional reflexes shaped by past pain. This is the moment where choice still exists—where awareness can interrupt the momentum.

Anger is Pre-Programmed

Most anger is not about the present at all. It's a **replay**—an old neural script. Your subconscious stores memories of emotional pain, and when similar triggers arise, it reacts on autopilot. In a split second, you find yourself trapped in a pattern: same reaction, same regret.

This is why anger can feel so immediate, even irrational. It's not *you* reacting—it's a **program.** And unless you rewire it, you'll keep repeating the same emotional loops.

Mindfulness is the Antidote

The only way to break free from these cycles is **mindfulness.** When you train your mind to stay present, you create a space between trigger and response. That space is where transformation begins.

You cannot wait for anger to arise to begin practicing mindfulness. The practice must be woven into the fabric of your daily life—when walking, eating, breathing, or simply observing your surroundings. These small moments of awareness are your training ground.

Over time, mindfulness weakens the grip of your old anger circuits. It allows the brain to **rewire** itself, shifting from reactive patterns to conscious responses.

Breaking the Cycle of Reaction

Even with the best intentions, we often relapse into old habits. You may vow to stay calm, yet explode the next time you're triggered. Why? Because without sustained awareness, your mind defaults to its **autopilot responses.**

Mindfulness helps you **catch the storm before it hits.** It sharpens your ability to feel the early tremors of anger—so you can step back, breathe, and respond with clarity rather than fury. In this way, you begin to **rewrite your emotional script.**

Make Mindfulness a Way of Living

Mindful living is not reserved for meditation mats or retreats. It must infiltrate your everyday life—your walk to work, your time with family, your pauses between tasks. With every small act of attention, you interrupt the mechanical patterns of reactivity.

In those sacred pauses, your choices become more aligned. You stop reacting to wounds and start responding from wisdom. This is how anger transforms—not into suppression or silence—but into **strength with compassion, firmness with grace.**

In Conclusion, Anger is Not the Enemy

Anger, at its core, is **pure energy.** When unconscious, it destroys. But when mastered, it fuels **growth, boundaries, transformation,** and even **healing.**

It is not about never getting angry—it is about learning to **stay awake within the fire.** With mindfulness, you begin to see anger not as something to fear or suppress, but as a **teacher**—pointing you toward wounds that need healing, truths that need speaking, and change that needs birthing.

When held with compassion and guided by awareness, your anger becomes not a weapon—but a **light.**

CHAPTER 24

CREATE WORLD CHANGE FROM INSIDE OUT

Q #24: I struggle with entrenched, smoldering resentment, judgment, and rage toward those who support evil politicians who blatantly lie, manipulate, ferment fear and oppression, and dismantle democracy. How do I deal with this?

When you are in a state of frustration, resentment, or rage, know that these are not *external* events—they are *internal storms.* These emotions are happening within *you*, not in the world. What I see in your words is the pain of someone who deeply cares, someone whose heart is breaking at the injustice around them.

But here's the key: your suffering is not because of a personal failure or loss—it's because you're sensitive to the world's suffering. You see people in positions of immense power—whether political or corporate—abusing it, manipulating minds, and exploiting fear. You feel helpless watching this, and naturally, the ego wants to fight, to resist, to rage.

Yet remember this sacred truth: **anger and resentment are not healing energies.** They are not the tools by which a better world is built. They cloud your mind, agitate your nervous system, and broadcast more negativity into a world already drowning in it.

If you truly want to see a better world, **your first responsibility is to preserve your inner poise and balance.** You cannot fight darkness by becoming dark within. You cannot heal through hatred.

Heal the World by Healing Within

Everything you wish to change outside—corrupt leadership, broken systems, unconscious masses—**must first be transformed inside you.** That means recognizing your anger, frustration, and judgment as invitations to grow in clarity, to choose a different inner state, and to release the suffering they cause.

When you release the resentment, you don't become passive—you become **powerfully aligned** with the higher intelligence of the universe. That intelligence *knows* how to bring about change in divine time and divine ways. But it needs **clear, open, peaceful instruments** to work through—and that's what you are being called to become.

At this moment, when you are radiating frustration and pain, **those vibrations are feeding the very energies you seek to counter.** Negative thoughts and feelings only amplify negative patterns in the collective. But when you rise above and choose compassion, prayer, and clarity, you contribute powerful waves of higher consciousness into the collective field.

How Real Change Happens: From the Inside Out

This is why we revere souls like Buddha, Christ, and the great sages. Their compassion and inner stability influenced not only the people around them but the very *energy* of the planet. You, too, have that potential.

Whatever you generate in your own being does **not remain contained**—it ripples outward.

So choose to generate **peace.**

Choose to generate **stillness.**

Choose to generate **a field of prayerful love.**

This is your **true activism**—subtle, powerful, and enduring.

Q: So, my pain and frustration, even though rooted in justice, are actually a threat to all that is good and positive in the world? So the central practice is to offer this anger to the Divine, to life itself, as a prayer for transformation?

Bodhi Answers: Precisely.

You've grasped the heart of the teaching.

You are speaking the language of energy. Whether we name them love, compassion, anger, fear, or rage—they are all energies. The question is: **which energy are you feeding?**

If you want to see transformation in the world—whether in politics, injustice, or systems of control—you **must** stop feeding the energies of resentment and rage within yourself. You cannot radiate suffering and expect peace to arise.

Your Anger Is a Signal, not a Solution

Instead of suppressing your pain, **offer it.** Imagine sending all that inner turbulence—your grief, your righteous anger, your broken heart—to the Divine like a signal to a satellite. Offer it to your **Guru**, to **God**, to **Life.** Let the Divine intelligence absorb it, transform it, and return to you waves of peace.

Then, sit quietly. Anchor yourself in silence. Let the **ripples of your inner peace** spread across the world like healing light.

Be a Beacon in a World of Storms

The world doesn't need more outrage. It needs more **light bearers.** More souls who remain centered amidst chaos. More hearts who radiate clarity instead of confusion. More beings whose inner life becomes a sanctuary for others.

And so, yes—**your central practice is surrender.**

Offer your pain and allow **compassion to arise.**

Offer your resentment, and let **forgiveness emerge.**

Offer your frustration, and become a **calm force for real change.**

This is the only way to help the world without being consumed by it.

Closing Reflection:

"You may not be able to stop all the evil in the world,
but you can stop it from taking root in your heart.
And when you do that, the light you become
will be part of what heals the world."

Let this be your practice. Let this be your path.

Let your heart be a place where suffering ends and healing begins.

CHAPTER 25

SPIRITUAL EVOLUTION: WHERE WE GO FROM HERE

Q#25: Where Do We Go from Here?

Mental health challenges are increasingly being recognized as a **modern epidemic.** Toxic parenting, emotional neglect, and unresolved childhood trauma are surfacing as widespread societal problems—manifesting in rising rates of **suicide, violence, depression, anxiety**, and growing **social dysfunction.** These issues are no longer personal; they are **collective wounds** that must be acknowledged, discussed, and healed—openly and globally.

We must begin by understanding that **ignoring anger** or suppressing it is not a viable solution. Instead, we need to learn how to **differentiate between healthy anger and unhealthy anger.**

- **Healthy anger** is *adaptive*; it serves as a signal that something is unjust or harmful and needs attention.

- **Unhealthy anger**—when it erupts as rage or fury—becomes *maladaptive*, distorting perception and leading to destruction, both internally and externally.

One of the deepest roots of this dysfunction is **toxic parenting**, often born from emotionally unavailable or chronically stressed parents. In modern "micro-family" units, parents are frequently overwhelmed—struggling to cope with work, finances, and emotional fatigue. In such settings, **devices often replace real presence**, and children are left emotionally unattended, fending for themselves in silence.

This emotional neglect during formative years breeds deep-seated insecurity and anger. Children, desperate for connection, validation, and love, often grow up learning that **expressing emotion is unsafe or unwelcome.** Particularly for boys, societal conditioning teaches that vulnerability is weakness. Emotional repression, then, becomes a learned survival skill—one that backfires in adulthood as mental health breakdowns, relational chaos, or even violence.

The Two-Pronged Solution

To address this epidemic, we need a **two-pronged approach:**

1. **Acknowledge the Roots of the Problem**
   We must go deeper than surface-level behavioral fixes. Healing must begin at the **root of the trauma**—which can start as early as **intrauterine stress**, continue through **neglectful parenting**, and be exacerbated by **shaming educational systems.**

Rather than labeling people as "angry" or "unstable," we must ask:

- **What unmet emotional needs lie beneath this outburst?**
- **What early wounds are surfacing now in dysfunctional forms?**

2. **Educate on Emotional Alchemy: Transforming Anger into Wisdom**
   The second path forward lies in teaching **the sacred art of transforming anger.** Every emotion is a **raw energy**—and anger is one of the most powerful. Left unchecked, it becomes destructive. But when understood, it becomes fuel for transformation.
   We need to equip **children, teens, and adults** with tools to transmute this fire into:
   - **Compassion**
   - **Forgiveness**
   - **Acceptance**
   - **Understanding**
   - **Love**

Practices like **mindfulness, breathwork, mantra (Japa), and meditation** allow individuals to pause, observe, and **redirect this powerful energy.** Over time, these practices help to **rewire the brain**, soothe the nervous system, and return the mind to a space of clarity and choice.

Healing the Future: What Society Must Embrace

If we truly want to transform society, we must also advocate for:

- **Conscious parenting education**, starting during pregnancy
- **Restoration of extended family networks** to support emotional nourishment
- **Integration of spiritual values** like empathy, humility, and kindness into mainstream education
- **Redefinition of masculinity** to include vulnerability, emotional expression, and inner strength
- **Cultural shift** away from glorifying violence and competition toward collaboration and harmony

This is not merely psychological work—it is **spiritual evolution.**

When we stop reacting and begin reflecting, when we stop blaming and begin understanding, we begin to **heal not only ourselves—but generations to come.**

ABOUT THE AUTHOR

SHUDDHAANANDAA BRAHMACHARI (BODHI)

Shuddhaanandaa Brahmachari (Bodhi) is a globally acclaimed motivational and inspirational speaker, author, spiritual teacher, humanitarian, and peacemaker. Founder of Stress Management Academy, his Simple Art of Managing Stress and Course in Mindfulness Programs are known worldwide, inspiring corporate leadership, students, and spiritual seekers alike. His current Breath for Oneness platform offers one-on-one, family, and group virtual and in-person spiritual and life-enhancing sessions.

He is recognized as a visionary humanitarian for his development of groundbreaking programs that serve thousands of poverty-stricken individuals in slums of Kolkata, India, and remote villages of West Bengal. He founded Lokenath Divine Life Mission in 1985. His self-authored books include: "Your Mind Your Best Friend", "Cleaning the Mirror of Mind", "Quintessence of Sai Satcharitra: A Biography of the Incredible Sai Baba of Shirdi", "The Incredible Life of a Himalayan Yogi: The Times, Teachings and Life of Living Shiva Baba Lokenath Brahmachari", "Meditations on Living Life: With Ascended Himalayan Master MahaYogi Baba Lokenath", "Sing, Chant, Love: Thakur's Treasure Trove of Practical Spirituality" and the inspirational biography of his Master: "Living with My Himalayan Master Sri Sri Bhajan Brahmachari—A Biography".

He was awarded the Man of Peace Award by the World Organization for Peace in 2012 in Mexico. He has spoken at the Parliament of World Religions, United Nations Global Youth Conference, and International Conference of Spiritualizing Leadership. He received a Lifetime Achievement Award from the S.T.A.R foundation at the House of Lords in the United Kingdom on July 21, 2015, for his invaluable and outstanding contribution to society.

www.bodhiguides.com

www.ingramcontent.com/pod-product-compliance
Lightning Source LLC
Chambersburg PA
CBHW050018170726
48282CB00025B/452
9788198286406